s, *Productivity, and Investment:*
ɪg *Financial Strategies in Higher Education*

, *Edward P. St. John*

ASHE-ERIC Higher Education Report No. 3, 1994

Prepared by

Clearinghouse on Higher Education
The George Washington University

In cooperation with

Association for the Study
of Higher Education

Published by

Graduate School of Education and Human Development
The George Washington University

Jonathan D. Fife, Series Editor

Cite as

St. John, Edward P. 1994. *Prices, Productivity, and Investment: Assessing Financial Strategies in Higher Education.* ASHE-ERIC Higher Education Report No. 3. Washington, D.C.: The George Washington University, School of Education and Human Development.

Library of Congress Catalog Card Number 94-73329
ISSN 0884-0040
ISBN 1-878380-59-1

Managing Editor: Bryan Hollister
Manuscript Editor: Barbara Fishel, Editech
Cover design by Michael David Brown, Rockville, Maryland

The ERIC Clearinghouse on Higher Education invites individuals to submit proposals for writing monographs for the *ASHE-ERIC Higher Education Report* series. Proposals must include:
1. A detailed manuscript proposal of not more than five pages.
2. A chapter-by-chapter outline.
3. A 75-word summary to be used by several review committees for the initial screening and rating of each proposal.
4. A vita and a writing sample.

ERIC Clearinghouse on Higher Education
School of Education and Human Development
The George Washington University
One Dupont Circle, Suite 630
Washington, DC 20036-1183

This publication was prepared partially with funding from the Office of Educational Research and Improvement, U.S. Department of Education, under contract no. ED RR-93-0200. The opinions expressed in this report do not necessarily reflect the positions or policies of OERI or the Department.

EXECUTIVE SUMMARY

Higher education is embroiled in a cost controversy that has eroded public confidence and taxpayers' financial support. Indeed, in many states the situation appears to have reached the level of crisis, with the new conditions negatively influencing the quality of academic life for faculty and students (Slaughter 1993a) and eroding opportunities for postsecondary education (Associated Press 1993). *Prices, Productivity and Investment* critically examines the cost controversy in higher education in an effort to build a better understanding of the types of financial strategies institutions and governments can use to help resolve the crisis in college costs.

Why Are College Costs Controversial?

The controversy over college costs first surfaced in the mid-1980s after a half decade of rising tuitions. The U.S. Congress mandated Secretary of Education William Bennett to conduct a study of college costs, focusing on why costs were increasing and how the federal government could maintain access and possibly mitigate future cost increases. The intent of Congress had been to focus on why the *prices* students paid were rising, but Secretary Bennett responded to the mandate by initiating studies that examined the growth in *educational expenditures* as an explanation for rising prices. Senior officials in the U.S. Department of Education also argued that student financial aid did not influence access or expenditures (Bennett 1986, 1987; Finn 1988a, 1988b). National associations responded to these claims by arguing that increases in tuition could be attributed to reductions in federal grants and state appropriations (Association of Governing Boards 1986; Council for Advancement 1987). During the past decade, the controversy over college costs has continued—and tuitions have continued to rise faster than inflation. In the face of mounting prices—and frequent articles in the popular press that claim (or imply) prices are increasing because of waste—taxpayers in many states have backed off their historic commitment to fund public higher education. Consequently, state subsidies to public higher education are actually declining (Hines 1993), at a time when enrollments are expected to be rising again (Gerald and Hussar 1990).

Did Federal Policies Contribute to the Controversy?

During the late 1970s and early 1980s, total federal expenditures for student grants declined, while the use of loans

expanded and the participation of minorities in higher education also declined. Senior officials in the Department of Education, however, adopted the philosophy that students did not respond to prices, and contractors with the Department who examined the causes of the decline in minority enrollments focused on deficiencies in the academic preparation of minority students but did not examine the possible influence of reductions in federal grants on minority enrollments (Pelavin and Kane 1988). Thus, the Department and its contractors ignored the fact that federal policies might have contributed to the decline in the participation rates of minorities, just as they had ignored the fact that these policies might have influenced rising tuitions.

Recent studies of the effects of federal student aid programs have documented that the shift from grants to loans in the 1980s directly influenced the downturn in the access of minorities to higher education and indirectly influenced the rate of growth in tuition, especially in private colleges. The reduction in grants influenced low-income and minority students to attend less expensive institutions or to delay their enrollment, although the increased emphasis on loans helped some middle-income students to attend, mitigating the effects of the shifts in federal student aid policy on total enrollments and disguising the negative effects of reductions in grants. Many private institutions used their own sources of revenue to substitute for the loss of federal grants. Thus, the changes in federal policy influenced the overall pattern of enrollment redistribution and indirectly influenced price increases in private colleges.

By the late 1980s, the erosion in federal grants and minorities' participation rates had apparently halted, but federal reports continued to claim institutions were responsible for rising costs and the controversy over college costs had spread to states.

Did State Policies Contribute to the Controversy?
During the early 1980s, the burden for financing public higher education shifted from states to students and their families (Kramer 1993a). An examination of the controversy acknowledged that institutions responded to reductions in state funding by raising tuition but claimed that increases in tuition did not influence enrollment (State Higher Education 1988). Periodic reductions in state support for higher education—

both for institutions and student grant programs—continued
through the 1980s. In the early 1990s, as total state support
for higher education actually declined (Hines 1993), many
public institutions were confronted with budget cuts. These
reductions in state support were apparently influenced only
by growing claims that institutions are excessive and wasteful.

This shift in the pattern of public finance of higher education has markedly influenced the controversy over costs.
First, the decline in state support has influenced tuitions in
the public sector to rise. Second, when most states cut appropriations to grant programs, they cut institutional appropriations, influencing a simultaneous increase in tuitions and
decrease in grants. Third, research indicates that these changes
contributed to the decline in the participation rates of minorities in the early 1980s (St. John 1991d, 1993b). Further, it
appears that access is also being eroded by the financial crisis
of the early 1990s.

Did Institutional Policies Contribute to the Controversy?
Throughout this period, national associations have focused
on how to tell their story about tuition increases. Their reports
encouraged institutions to point out how state and federal
policies influenced increases in tuition and the improvements
in quality they were making in the services they provide to
undergraduates (Association of Governing Boards 1986; Council for Advancement 1987; National Institute 1987). Most associations and many institutional officials dismissed the claim
that inefficiencies contributed to rising tuitions.

Why have prices increased? The research on college
costs has identified three reasons for increases in tuition during the past 14 years. First, federal student aid policies have
influenced many private colleges to raise tuition to generate
more revenue for grants (Hauptman 1990a, 1990b). Second,
states have shifted a larger share of the burden for financing
public colleges and universities to students and their families,
which has influenced public tuitions to rise (Kramer 1993a).
Third, an incremental increase in educational expenditures
also contributed to rising costs (Getz and Siegfried 1991).

The increases in expenditures had three primary causes.
First, instructional expenditures increased in the early 1980s
as a result of increases in faculty salaries, an adjustment for
the late 1970s, when faculty salaries lagged behind inflation.
In the past decade, instructional expenditures grew about

as fast as inflation. Second, administrative expenditures increased faster than inflation throughout the 1980s and early 1990s because of growth in administrative salaries, increases in the numbers of administrators, and increases in their professionalization. Some of these changes have helped to generate other revenues and thus keep tuition lower than it might have been without institutions' recent changes in their academic and enrollment management strategies. Other aspects of the growth in administration, however, apparently caused prices (tuitions and other student charges) to increase. Third, higher education has absorbed new technologies, such as computers and telecommunications, without reducing its production costs.

Has higher education's productivity changed? The basic production functions influencing instructional costs—student/faculty ratios, average class sizes, and so forth—changed very little during the past decades. While attempts to measure productivity in higher education historically have been fraught with problems in measurement, however, it is also evident that faculty and administrators have few incentives to adopt more productive behavior. Faculty are rewarded for their productivity in research rather than in teaching. And administrators are rewarded based on their portfolios—the number of programs and staff they manage—rather than for their efficiency. Thus, the instructional productivity of colleges and universities has gradually eroded during the second half of the 20th century, and this gradual change influenced increases in tuition. It is therefore crucial that the internal incentive structure within colleges and universities be considered when strategies aimed at improving productivity are devised.

Is higher education a good investment? Higher education is a good investment for students, and the financial returns on an individual's investment are substantial. Further, if tax revenue is considered as a return on government investment, then it appears that federal student aid has a substantial return to the federal government—more than four dollars for every dollar spent (St. John and Masten 1990). And it appears that state expenditures on higher education bring a substantial return in tax revenues in states that have progressive tax systems (Bluestone 1993; Girling, Goldman, and Keith 1993) and a positive return in states with regressive tax systems (Creech, Carpenter, and Davis 1994). Tax revenue returns by themselves, however, provide a poor basis for arguing that more should be spent (Kramer 1993a), especially if the historic problems with productivity continue to be ignored.

Can the Negative Effects of Price Increases be Reduced?

Throughout the past decade, this question, which Congress raised when it mandated that the Secretary of Education conduct a study of college costs, has largely gone unaddressed. Research on the effects of recent changes in financial strategy in higher education provides some insight, however. Middle-income students responded positively to the increased emphasis on loans in the 1980s, while loans per se had little influence on low-income and minority enrollments. Low-income students were negatively influenced by tuition charges and positively influenced by grants. When tuitions increased and grants declined in the early 1980s, minority participation rates also declined, especially for African-Americans. Therefore, emphasizing loans could be more cost-effective to the federal government than placing a heavy emphasis on grants, if the negative effects of loans are minimized for low-income students. Thus, the federal government should make a more consistent and concerted effort to monitor the effects of its policy changes on access than it has since the mid-1970s.

It is possible that the high-tuition, high-grant strategy would maintain the enrollment of low-income students if states used the strategy. Unfortunately, states cut grants as well as institutional appropriations when they are confronted with tax revenue shortfalls. Thus, a more concerted effort to increase grants when institutional appropriations are cut could help maintain access if the burden for financing public institutions continues to shift toward students. Evidence also exists, however, that high tuition in public institutions can increase the time it takes for students to complete their degrees, which means that a high-tuition, high-aid strategy could marginally reduce productivity.

Further, institutions should explicitly consider the effects of price increases when they set their tuition and grant policies each year. During the past 15 years, private colleges and universities used the reallocation of some tuition revenues to student grants as a means of maintaining enrollments. The number of institutions could be limited that can adopt high-tuition, high-aid strategies without eroding total enrollments and degree attainment, and institutions should therefore routinely assess the effects of their pricing decisions on enrollment and degree completion.

Can Productivity Be Improved?

The cost controversy has cast a shadow of blame and doubt over higher education. Colleges and universities were criticized for being greedy and unproductive, when their productivity has changed relatively little over time. Higher education, unlike private industry, has historically absorbed new technologies without improving productivity. A substantial turnover in faculty should occur during the next ten years as massive numbers of faculty hired in the 1960s and early 1970s retire. This turnover and the new technologies available in theory create opportunities for improving productivity.

Successful efforts to improve productivity in higher education, however, should consider the internal incentive structure in the academic community. Recent efforts to centralize academic strategy have not increased the incentives for faculty to experiment with new approaches to instructional productivity. Increased decentralization of financial strategy might be necessary to create incentives for more faculty to experiment with approaches to instruction that improve educational outcomes (meaningful gains in productivity) as a means of improving the affordability of college. Colleges and universities should consider pay incentives for improvements in instructional productivity. In this environment, faculty, students, *and* taxpayers can benefit from these gains in productivity. If the incentive structure can be appropriately modified, then it is possible that a new form of professional responsibility could emerge.

Questions related to the causes and consequences of rising administrative costs merit closer examination within colleges and universities and within government agencies. Recent studies paint two types of pictures: one of administrative excesses contributing to rising tuitions, the other of increasing professionalization in administrative services helping higher education to avert the financial disaster that was predicted for the 1980s. Both accounts probably contain some truth and fiction, and questions related to administrative productivity and efficiency should therefore be more thoughtfully and thoroughly examined.

States and the federal government can facilitate movement toward a new incentive structure. They can support and conduct institutional peer cost studies, encourage experiments aimed at reducing instructional and administrative costs, and openly assess the effects of their financing strategies on institutions.

Can Returns on Higher Education Be Improved?

A central issue facing the academic community is whether the returns on investment can be improved. In other words, having good returns might no longer be sufficient rationale for justifying public support, given that a shrinking percentage of the population can afford the full direct costs of higher education. Further, the fact that students have high returns might not help institutions in marketing when students are confronted by high levels of personal debt. Therefore, states and the federal government are confronted by questions about how to optimize the strategies they use to finance higher education. And institutions are confronted by very basic questions about whether they can improve returns through improvements in productivity. These questions merit the attention of the academic and policy communities.

CONTENTS

FOREWORD

How much it costs to attend a higher education institution
directly affects the type of people it serves, the quality of education it provides, and how well it can achieve its mission.
The pricing of education is a result of five interrelated areas:
a consideration of costs relative to the people being served,
a philosophical approach to costs as related to the costs of
other "peer" institutions, the culture of the institution con-
cerning the use of available resources, actual costs, and the
consequences of decisions made in other parts of the system.
Every individual concerned with higher education in general
or with a particular institution can influence pricing decisions
or the responses to pricing decisions.

The first two aspects of pricing can be seen in how academic leaders interpret the educational mission of institutions
and consequently the institutions that they see as their primary competitors. If the mission is to serve the economically
disadvantaged, then it is likely that everything possible will
be done to maintain low tuition. If the approach, however,
is to see the institution within a certain tuition stratum, as
represented by institutions that are also attractive to their student applicants or institutions that they would like to be compared to, the pricing strategy will be highly influenced by the
other institutions' tuition. The problem with these two
approaches to pricing is that neither is based on real costs
or real educational outcomes. And because they lack reality,
the possibility exists that income will not be high enough
to meet expenses or that tuition costs will appear to be unre-
lated to educational results.

The third influence on pricing is the institution's culture—
the values represented in the system of allocating resources.
While a few exceptions exist, most units in a higher education
institution measure their success by being able to spend all,
if not most, of their budgets, based on a combination of the
quest for excellence and fear of losing finite and scarce
resources. Underlying this reasoning, justified by the quest
for quality, are three other basic beliefs. Resources are perceived as finite and prestige is therefore measured by how
much money is allocated to a unit. Accompanying the belief
of finite resources is a belief that resources, represented by
an annual budget, are scarce and limited and that it is therefore better to spend them all now because the future might
not be as generous. The win-lose belief is reflected in the attitude that if the budget is not fully depleted, the balance will

go to someone else, who will then have more money than you—they win, you lose. Thus, it is seen as a sign of good management to spend all the money in the budget to ensure maximum resources for a unit.

The result of decisions based on the quest for excellence and the philosophy of scarcity is that budgets and spending are so inflated that it becomes difficult to determine the actual or minimal costs an institution needs to meet to achieve the overall educational mission and, therefore, at what level education should be priced. The movement toward quality management and the practice of benchmarking, that is, comparing the outcomes to costs of other institutions, offer some hope. By comparing other institutions' outcomes and expenses, it is possible to identify exemplary institutions that seem to have a more effective outcomes-to-expenses ratio that can be studied and, where appropriate, imitated.

The fifth condition affecting pricing is the most important—the resulting consequences of decisions made in other parts of the system. A conspicuous example is the federal government's decisions affecting student financial aid and their results on the pricing of independent higher education. During the 1980s, federal funding for student aid decreased per recipient, was based more on need, and moved to stronger reliance on loans. As a consequence, private or independent institutions had to provide more student aid to have a socioeconomically balanced student body, greatly increasing expenses and causing tuition to rise. A second example of the consequences on costs of decisions in other parts of the system is the lack of incentives normally provided for a unit to stay within its budget. Decisions to take back all unspent money or reduce future budgets based on the logic that a budget underspent is a sign of an inflated budget establishes an incentive to spend funds regardless of need.

Decisions affecting pricing, productivity, and investment in higher education will be even more critical in the future. Edward P. St. John, professor of educational leadership at the University of New Orleans, addresses the issues related to these decisions in depth in this ASHE-ERIC Higher Education Report. He first reviews the implications of financing strategies from federal and state perspectives, then turns to institutional strategies and the complex issue of productivity. Building his conclusions on four theories that influence financial strategies—human capital theory, revenue theory, political incrementalism, and critical theory—St. John proposes a number of financial strategies that should be considered in future pricing decisions.

The cost and pricing of higher education are the results of the collective actions and decisions of almost everyone who participates in higher education. All need to become aware of the consequences of their actions on prices and accept responsibility for the results. This report will help to understand how our actions influence pricing and provide ways to live more consciously of these consequences.

Jonathan D. Fife
Series Editor, Professor, and
Director, ERIC Clearinghouse on Higher Education

ACKNOWLEDGMENTS

Many people have helped me develop an understanding of higher education policy and finance. Those who have influenced this work, through their interest, support, and questioning include Mary Regan, James Meyer, George Weathersby, Greg Jackson, Fred Jacobs, James Farmer, Bill Goggin, Jay Noell, James Hearn, Don Hossler, John Smart, Michael Paulsen, Sandy Andrieu, Pat Somers, Johnny Starkey, Wilma Longstreet, and Daryl Hippensteel. Their questions and insights have been a great help in my efforts to develop a perspective and a way of viewing the financial conditions we face as students, faculty, and policy analysts. While I think there is room, and indeed even a need, for differences of opinion about the financial and educational issues that we face, I also believe that we need to develop shared understandings that can provide a basis for an informed conversation. These colleagues have helped me in my efforts to become part of such a conversation.

Additionally, the reviewers of the proposal and draft of this study were extremely helpful in bringing the issues I was grappling with into clearer focus. And I would especially like to acknowledge the support of Angela St. John, who helped with the production of this study. All of these contributions are gratefully acknowledged; however, the opinions expressed here are mine and should not be interpreted as representing the viewpoints of those who have influenced my work through their friendship, support, or review.

INTRODUCTION

During the past decade, the higher education community has been embroiled in a controversy over college costs. Each year when higher tuitions are announced, the popular press criticizes the apparent excessiveness of higher education. College and university administrators in turn justify the price increases on grounds of improved quality, cuts in state support, cuts in federal student grants, and increases in the costs of technology. This annual public trial is an event in which higher education generally has not fared well. The widespread perception, communicated routinely in the popular press and on radio talk shows, is that colleges and universities are excessive, wasteful, poorly managed, and of poor quality.

This annual public trial is an event in which higher education generally has not fared well.

Lurking beneath the surface of this popular criticism of higher education is a complex set of financial issues that should be of concern to—and the subject of debate within— the entire higher education community. The fact is that higher education in the United States is in financial trouble—and is headed for even more serious problems. While the emergence of strategic planning and management (Chaffee 1985, 1989; Keller 1983; Norris and Poulton 1987) and of enrollment management (Hossler 1984, 1987; Hossler, Bean, and Associates 1990) in the 1980s helped academe avert the predicted decline in enrollments, these developments also unleashed a set of fundamental changes in financing strategy that have become serious problems for the entire higher education community. The controversy over costs has made the public less willing to dedicate tax dollars to support colleges and universities and students and their families less willing to pay the full costs of attending college. Given that these deeper issues have gone unaddressed, the controversy over costs is reaching crisis proportions.

Understanding the Cost Controversy

The controversy over college costs is only the tip of a complex set of financial problems facing the higher education community. The controversy centered initially around rising tuition. Congress mandated in the Education Amendments of 1985 that the secretary of education conduct a study of college costs, focusing on discovering the causes of rising prices and ways that states and the federal government could minimize the impact of rising prices on lower- and middle-income families. If the language of the legislation had been interpreted from a "liberal" perspective, it automatically would have been assumed that federal financial support could constrain future increases in price.

A liberal interpretation of congressional intent was inconsistent with the beliefs of the Reagan administration, however, especially the intellectual leaders of the U.S. Department of Education, Secretary William Bennett and Assistant Secretary Chester Finn. The administration had been proposing annual cuts to federal grant programs and increases in loans, based on a belief that the financing of higher education was an individual rather than a public responsibility. Bennett claimed that colleges and universities had raised their prices to increase their revenue from federal student aid programs (1986), while Finn charged that colleges and universities were excessive and wasteful (1988a). These claims ignited a controversy that has had far-reaching implications.

The higher education community immediately responded by making counterclaims of its own. Independent colleges and universities claimed prices had risen because of cuts in federal student aid (National Institute 1987), public colleges claimed the price increases were attributable to cuts in state subsidies (Eiser 1988), and trustee organizations focused on methods of selling price increases to the public (Council for Advancement 1987). The popular press also carried these counterclaims, but although articulate spokespeople led the defense, their message did not sell well with the popular press (see, e.g., Putka 1987).

The popular belief contributed to the problem confronting the academic community:

The escalation in college costs is occurring because it enables the people who run colleges to extract profits from an ostensibly nonprofit system and redistribute them as they wish. . . . Washington's shift to "need-based" programs in the late 1970s effectively allowed higher educators to tap federal funds simply by raising their fees (Brimelow 1987, p. 148).

The older beliefs about the economic and human value of higher education were no longer commonly held (Simsek and Heydinger 1992).

Comments about a recent report by the American Council on Education that describes colleges' and universities' efforts to adjust to the more stressful conditions of the early 1990s illustrate how pervasive this critical attitude toward higher education has become.

*Universities expanded for a long time, and it's hard to break
the habit. But governance changes and reorganizations
won't help much if schools can't face squarely that their
operations cost more than they can currently afford
(Washington Post 1994).*

These comments, in a newspaper often characterized as being
part of the liberal press, illustrate quite clearly that institutional "excesses" are now generally thought to be the primary
cause of the financial problems facing higher education.

Other more complex issues linger beneath the surface of
the controversy about costs. Regardless of the political—or
ideological—spin put on the developments in higher education finance, an apparent financial restructuring[1] occurred
in the 1980s. Further, that financial restructuring has influenced an increase in the percentage of costs paid for by students and their families (Kramer 1993a). The federal government reduced its funding of need-based grants (Lewis 1989),
private colleges used a portion of its gains in tuition revenues
to increase grants (Hauptman 1990a, 1990b), and the percentage of educational and related costs in public colleges and
universities that states subsidized through direct appropriations declined (St. John 1992a). Whether a causal link existed
between changes in federal student aid policy and state-level
financial restructuring was seldom examined. The neoconservatives used escalated prices as evidence to support their
arguments about institutional excessiveness (e.g., Finn 1988a),
while national associations argued that increases in tuition
were caused by changes in federal policy (e.g., Council for
Advancement 1987; National Institute 1987). The fact that
higher education was in the middle of a financial restructuring
was often overlooked.

This process of financial restructuring—basic changes in
the way colleges and universities are financed—has continued
into the 1990s, accompanied by the increased regularity of
state budget rescissions (Hines 1993) and resulting reductions
in student enrollments (see, e.g., Associated Press 1993).
These financial cutbacks, largely unanticipated by financial

---

1. "Financial restructuring" here refers to the basic changes in the structure
of higher education finance. "Restructuring" has been more frequently used
to refer to basic changes in curricula and academic organization, a process
referred to here as "academic restructuring."

analysts in colleges and universities, were experienced as *retrenchment*—the systematic process of reducing operating expenses and faculty and staff positions. Some critical theorists have begun to examine the issues of class embedded in these battles over retrenchment (Gumport 1993; Rhoades 1993; Slaughter 1993a, 1993b), but the link between retrenchment and longer-term financial restructuring has been less frequently examined.

In the midst of this complexity, the role of financial strategy—the actual financial choices government agencies and institutions of higher education made during financial restructuring—has received very little attention. While some speculated that changes in prices did not influence enrollment (see, e.g., Hansen 1983; State Higher Education 1988), it appears that financial restructuring did affect the distribution of enrollments (Pascarella, Smart, and Smylie 1992)—suggesting that a link existed between financial decisions and enrollments and that the link was clouded over by changing political ideologies.

The Influence of Political Ideologies

The election of Ronald Reagan in 1980 signaled more than a shift back to a Republican presidency after four years of Democratic leadership. It also signaled the end of 15 years of building and refining Great Society programs, including the Higher Education Act of 1965's Title IV (student aid) programs. The beginning of the Reagan administration symbolized the end of widely held beliefs that the federal government had an important role to play in promoting equal educational opportunity.

With the breakdown in the liberal progressive consensus that public investment in higher education promoted social and economic progress (Simsek and Heydinger 1992)—and in bipartisan congressional support for federal student aid programs—attention to the role of political belief systems, or ideologies, has become much more crucial to building an understanding of the consequences of choices about financial strategy in higher education. When a community operates within a widely held political belief system, it tends not to examine its embedded (ideological) claims, but rather to use available evidence to support its political agendas (Argyris, Putnam, and Smith 1985; Habermas 1984, 1987; Lindblom and Cohen 1979). When neoconservatives began to take a critical look at student aid programs in the early 1980s, they began to seriously question progressive liberal claims about equal opportunity and social progress. They also introduced a new set of beliefs—that federal programs (and by extension higher education) contained waste, fraud, and abuse—that they never seriously questioned.

These new beliefs, which rapidly became pervasive in the federal policy arena, profoundly influenced the emergence of the controversy over college costs. To untangle the pervasive influence that ideologies have on policy, it is necessary to identify and assess the claims made within these belief systems. In higher education, the claims of five ideologies are pertinent (see table 1).

The original conservative argument was that, *because the benefits of investment in higher education accrued primarily to individuals, its costs should be subsidized by students and their families, rather than government.* Before World War II, states subsidized postsecondary education by maintaining low tuition (institutional subsidies) at public institutions. But the federal government had played a more modest role, aimed primarily at specially directed programs that were in the federal interest, a strategy consistent with conventional conservative tenets. Stated in the extreme, conservatives believed:

> *Public expenditures on higher education can be justified as a means of training youngsters for citizenship and for community leadership . . . [, but] restricting the subsidy to schooling obtained in a state school cannot be justified on any grounds. Any subsidy should be granted to individuals to be spent at institutions of their own choosing, providing only that the schooling is of a kind that is desired to be subsidized* (Friedman 1962, p. 99).

In other words, extreme conservatives argued that government should not play a role in directly subsidizing institutions. Rather, these subsidies should be portable, enabling students to choose their own education.

At the time this argument was made, the pattern of state investment—subsidizing tuition through direct institutional appropriations—was well established. This argument would seem to have been a basis for arguing against expanding a federal role in subsidizing higher education institutions, a subject of political debate at the time.

TABLE 1

A FRAMEWORK FOR CRITICALLY EXAMINING IDEOLOGICAL CLAIMS

Ideology	Claim	Addressed in:*
Conservative	• Returns from the public investment accrue primarily to individuals	"Federal," "State"
Liberal	• Economic development and intergenerational equity provide bases for public investment	"Federal," "State"
Neoconservative	• Student aid has no influence on access	"Federal," "State," "Institutional"
	• Institutions raise tuition to increase revenue from federal aid programs	"State," "Institutional"
	• Institutions raise tuition to maximize revenue (greed)	"State," "Institutional"
	• Institutions raise tuition because they are unproductive	"State," "Institutional"
	• Poor academic achievement explains lower participation by African-Americans	"Federal"
Neoliberal	• Institutions replace the loss of federal student aid dollars with their own aid dollars, which influence tuition increases	"State," "Institutional"
	• Reductions in state subsidies to institutions fuel tuition increases	"State"
	• Tax revenue returns provide a basis for public investment	"State," "Institutional"
Neo-Marxist	• Low-income and minority students are negatively influenced by the entire cost controversy	"Federal," "State"
	• Programs serving middle-class majors are more adversely influenced by budget rescissions than programs serving elite professions	"State"

* "Federal," "State," and "Institutional" refer to the next three sections, titled, respectively, "Federal Financing Strategies," "State Financing Strategies," and "Institutional Financing Strategies."

The liberal argument about expanding the federal role in education was based on the idea that *the federal government could expand, indeed "equalize," educational opportunity.* Human capital theory provided a logical basis for this argument. A relationship existed between educational costs and the opportunity to attend, with federal loans (at the time, National Defense Education Loans were generally available) reducing the costs for individuals and expanding opportunity (Becker 1964). Between the middle 1960s and the late 1970s, the federal role in supporting student aid expanded rapidly. The liberal argument was essentially that this "intergenerational transfer" (with funds following students) could improve "intergenerational equity" (Kramer 1993a, p. 20). Assessing the social benefits of this investment, however, became a complicated issue, at least if the human capital paradigm were maintained:

> *For some kinds of investigations in human capital theory, it is important to distinguish returns [attributed] to the skills acquired through higher education—that is, the actual increment in productivity—from returns [attributed to] a degree or other credential. . . . The greater income of someone with an educational credential is clearly a private benefit* (Kramer 1993a, p. 13).

This line of reasoning provides two bases on which to judge the benefits of the public investment in education—growth in the gross national product and improvements in cross-generational equity, both of which were identified in the original statement of human capital theory (Becker 1964). This line of reasoning, which proponents of increased government support frequently used (Slaughter 1991), was applied to both the state investment in tuition subsidies (through direct appropriations) and to the federal investment in student aid. Unfortunately, when policy studies adhered to these tenets, the benefits of the taxpayers' investment were difficult to estimate (Kramer 1993a). And this difficulty with measuring the benefits of the public investment has made government expenditures more difficult to defend in the face of federal and state efforts to reduce taxes and public expenditures.

For the neoconservatives, those who argued for returning to a prior state of society when tax dollars were not used so extensively to support social programs aimed at promoting equity (Habermas 1992; St. John and Elliott 1994), the liberal constraints on the means that could appropriately be used to assess the effects of government investment were not treated as valid. And the arguments developed by neoconservatives in the 1980s created particularly difficult obstacles for those who held liberal tenets. Five of these arguments are summarized in the following paragraphs.

First, neoconservatives argued that *student aid was not effective in promoting access.* The foundations for this argument were laid in a study comparing participation rates for students in the high school classes of 1972 and 1980 as a means of assessing the effects of increased expenditures on federal Title IV programs (Hansen 1983). But "the programs did little or nothing to promote their most important goal—increased access . . . [—and] it appears therefore that this set of redistributive programs produced little or no effect at a considerable cost and may well have contributed to the slowing of economic growth in recent years" (Hansen 1983, pp. 95, 96). Despite other evidence that student aid had a positive effect on access (e.g., Manski and Wise 1983), this argument received much attention in the U.S. Department of Education.

Second, neoconservatives claimed that *institutions raised their tuition to attract more federal student aid.* Bennett, secretary of education at the time, was the proponent of this argument. The essence of his argument was that increasing student aid does not help needy students cope with college costs, because the main effect of aid is simply to cause schools to raise their prices (Bennett 1986). This claim extended beyond the conclusion that student aid is not effective in promoting access by adding the claim that its *main* effect was to raise prices.

Third, neoconservatives claimed that *colleges and universities raised their prices out of greed.* "Some of our colleges and universities charge what the market will bear. . . . And lately they have found that it will bear quite a lot, indeed" (W.J. Bennett, quoted in H. Anderson 1987, p. 66; see also Bennett 1987). Bruce Carnes, deputy under secretary of education, agreed: "The governing principle of colleges today is to raise as much money as they can, and to spend as much money as they can" (quoted in Putka 1987, p. 27). This line of argument, loosely based on Bowen's revenue theory (1980), provided a logical basis for linking arguments about student aid to criticisms about the intent of college and university administrators and the lack of productivity by faculty. While Bowen had argued that, in quest of excellence, prestige, and influence, virtually no limit exists on the amount of money colleges and universities could spend (1980), Bennett and other neoconservatives reinterpreted this claim to argue that the motive for generating revenue was greed rather than excellence.

Fourth, neoconservatives argued that *colleges were wasteful and unproductive, another reason for raising prices.* Chester Finn, assistant secretary for research and improvement and the most articulate spokesperson for this neoconservative position, argued: "Our institutions aren't nearly so efficient or productive as they should be—and are getting less so" (1988b, p. 36). Finn was particularly effective at amassing evidence in support of the administration's arguments that a decline in productivity—by administrators and faculty—was the primary reason for rising tuition charges (Finn 1988a, 1988b).

Fifth, after the Reagan administration was confronted with a downturn in participation rates of minorities, it argued that *the poor academic preparation of minorities was the primary cause* of this development—the logical extension of the other claims about higher education finance. If student aid were ineffective in promoting equal access, then cuts in student grants could not be the cause of the downturn in participation rates of minorities. This argument was advanced by the administration's contractors, policy research firms that used studies to support the administration's positions. A study conducted for the Department of Education's Office of Planning, Budget, and Evaluation was one of the first to make the claim:

> *A primary reason that relatively fewer lower-achieving blacks enroll in college is that relatively fewer lower-achieving students in high school go on to college, and black high school students have, on average, lower achievement than white students* (Chaikind ca. 1987, p. 2).

These arguments were exceedingly difficult for liberals in the higher education community to contend with, given their belief that the benefits of the public investment accrued through gains in national productivity and in intergenerational equity. Three counterarguments, emerging partially in response to neoconservative claims, provide a basis for an emergent neoliberal ideology. Neoliberalism is characterized here as an emerging ideology aimed at rebuilding taxpayers' investment. It is, in a sense, a reconstructed set of liberal beliefs aimed at regaining lost ground.

First, neoliberals argued that *institutions have replaced losses in federal grants with their own grant allocations, a devel-*

opment that has fueled price increases. This argument, made
in expert congressional testimony (Green 1987) and literature
produced by national associations (Hauptman and Hartle
1987; National Institute 1987), appears in one sense to be the
opposite of Bennett's claim that student aid fueled price
increases. Nevertheless, it raised the possibility that the indirect effect of reductions in federal grants was to fuel price
increases. And the surface indicators, rising tuition and declining federal grants in the 1980s (Hauptman and Hartle 1987;
Lewis 1989), seemed to support this contention. To determine
whether these developments were coincidental or causal,
however, analysts had to look beneath descriptive trends.

Second, neoliberals, particularly in associations of public
colleges and universities, claimed that *reductions in state support had fueled the escalation in prices* (Atwell and Hauptman
1986; Eiser 1988). The wavering of state support for public
higher education is now well documented (see, e.g., Associated Press 1993; Hines 1988, 1993), but the implications
of this shift in the structure of higher education finance merit
fuller exploration (e.g., Hauptman 1993; Hauptman and Roose
1993; Kramer 1993b).

Third, it has recently been argued that *substantial tax
revenue accrues from the government's investment in higher
education.* While from a traditional liberal perspective this
approach essentially falls into the "trap of double counting,"
at least when gains in productivity are considered as a measure of benefit (Kramer 1993a), it does provide a better basis
for contending with neoconservative claims than the more
traditional measures of impact. Those who advocate this
approach construct a cost/benefit ratio of tax expenditures
on the cost side and tax revenue returns attributable to this
expenditure on the benefit side (Levin 1983). The approach
has been used to assess both state and federal investments
(Bluestone 1993; Girling, Goldman, and Keith 1993; St. John
and Masten 1990).

With the swings in traditional political belief systems, it is
possible to overlook the poor and minority populations, the
"historically disadvantaged" who were the original target for
federal student aid. Neo-Marxist political philosophy provides
another basis for assessing the effects of federal, state, and
institutional decisions about financing higher education. Marx-
ism essentially argues that as a result of the class dialectic,
the lower class is systematically oppressed by the upper class.

The dialectic provides a basis for examining how changes in policy differentially influence different groups. It emphasizes how the political economy—the interests of corporations and the wealthy—influences the distribution and redistribution of resources and the consequences of these processes. The recent literature on higher education provides two sets of neo-Marxist claims that merit consideration in the debates over higher education finance.

First, it has been argued that *cuts in federal grant programs had negatively affected participation rates of African-Americans and Hispanics* (Wilson 1986), an argument that holds embedded neo-Marxist tenets. This argument was made in an effort to raise public awareness of the potential negative effects of cuts in student aid. The initial studies on the decline in minority participation rates sponsored by the Reagan administration (Chaikind ca. 1987; Pelavin and Kane 1988, 1990) and associations of state higher education executives (Mingle 1987) deemphasized the link between minority enrollment and financing strategies and instead focused on academic preparation. Other recent research, however, has established a link between changes in policies about aid and participation of minorities (Mortensen 1987; St. John 1991d; St. John and Noell 1989). Thus, in retrospect, the initial studies diverted attention from considering the impact of changes in student aid policy and thus may have been purposeful deceptions.

Second, it has been argued that *majors serving middle-class students are victims of retrenchment,* another argument based on neo-Marxist tenets. Recent critical studies of retrenchment in higher education have documented that when institutions find it necessary to cut faculty positions, majors that serve middle-class students (and especially major programs that serve mostly females, like nursing and education) are more likely to be cut than majors that serve elite professions (Gumport 1993; Slaughter 1993a, 1993b). Further, it appears that the reasons "middle-class majors" are the hardest hit during retrenchment are that programs that serve elite professions (engineering, computer science, business) have close ties to powerful constituencies in the local economies where colleges and universities are located (Slaughter 1993a, 1993b); and that such programs are generally more closely aligned with institutions' strategic aims (St. John 1993a), a condition influenced by the power of departments that attract large amounts of external funds (Pfeffer and Moore 1980).

The wavering of state support for public higher education is now well documented.

A Critical Review

This study undertakes a critical review of recent developments in financial strategy in higher education. It examines research on higher education finance to assess the validity of the ideological claims summarized in table 1 about higher education finance and to construct an alternative way of thinking about the evolution and development of financial strategy in higher education. The study has two aims: to assess the effects of changes in federal, state, and institutional financing strategies of the past 15 years as a means of gaining insight into our current predicament; and to assess the likely effects of alternative financial strategies, focusing on steps that faculty, administrators, and public officials can take in their efforts to deal with the crisis in college costs. The next three sections critically examine recent trends and research on the roles of the federal government, state governments, and institutional administrators, respectively, in higher education finance and then reflect on whether the research supports related ideological claims. The last two sections reexamine the theories commonly used in the study of higher education finance, reconstruct a framework that can be used in analyses of financial strategies, and then use the reconstructed framework to assess strategies for reducing costs of production and making college more affordable.

FEDERAL FINANCING STRATEGIES

The federal government's primary role in the financing of higher education is to promote equity through generally available, need-based financial aid programs, authorized under Title IV of the Higher Education Act (HEA), as amended. Title IV programs were reorganized in 1972 to meet three goals (Gladieux and Wolanin 1976; National Commission on the Financing 1973): *access* (the opportunity to attend), *choice of school* (the opportunity to attend the school students are qualified to attend), and *persistence* (the opportunity to continue enrollment in the school of choice to the extent of interest and ability rather than of money). These three behaviors—deciding to attend college (or other postsecondary schooling), choosing a college or university, and persisting—in combination are characterized as "student choice behavior." This section critically examines the effects on student choice behavior of recent changes in federal policy regarding student aid. First, it examines research on the federal role in subsidizing college prices, focusing on the direct effects of student aid on student enrollment behavior. Second, it reviews the emerging federal role in promoting productivity in higher education, including evidence related to the quality of the delivery of student aid and recent federal efforts to promote institutional productivity. Third, it discusses the federal role in subsidizing students through federal student aid programs, viewing it as an investment. And, finally, it considers the implications of this review in relation to recent ideological claims.

The Federal Role in Pricing

Loans and other forms of student aid reduce an individual's direct costs of attending school (Becker 1964). Accordingly, federal student aid programs can be viewed as a price subsidy that promotes the attainment of higher education. This discussion considers both the recent changes in federal student aid programs and the evolving impact of those programs.

The evolving federal role

Table 2 reviews trends in the amounts of funds available through all federal programs between FY 1971 and FY 1990. First, based on an examination of only Title IV programs (part I of the table), it appears that the growth in student aid has been constant and substantial. Total aid available through Title IV programs increased throughout the period. In FY 1971, funding for Title IV loans was substantially higher than for

TABLE 2

TRENDS IN FINANCIAL AID AWARDED THROUGH FEDERAL STUDENT AID PROGRAMS, FYs 1971, 1976, 1981, 1986, 1990 (Millions of 1990 Dollars)

	70-71	75-76		80-81		85-86		89-90	
	Amount	Amount	% Change	Amount	% Change	Amount	% Change	Amount	% Change
I. *Generally Available Student Aid (HEA, Title IV)*									
• *Grants*									
Pell	$ 0	$2,301	NA	$3,755	63	$4,469	19	$ 5,116	14
SEOG	458	494	8	579	17	514	−11	478	−7
SSIG	0	48	NA	114	138	95	−17	77	−19
Subtotal	$458	$2,843	521	$4,448	56	$5,078	14	$ 5,671	12
• *Work*									
CWS	$780	$725	−7	$1,039	43	$822	−21	$712	−13
• *Loans*									
Perkins	$ 825	$1,130	37	$ 1,090	−3	$ 881	−19	$ 968	10
ICL	0	0	NA	0	NA	0	NA	6	NA
Guaranteed	3,482	3,113	−11	9,757	213	11,073	13	13,038	18
Subtotal	$4,307	$4,243	−1	$10,847	156	$11,954	10	$14,012	17
II. *Specially Directed Student Aid (Other Legislation)*									
• *Grants*									
Social Security	$1,712	$ 2,686	57	$2,962	10	$ 0	−100	$ 0	NA
Veteran	3,846	10,270	167	2,697	−74	1,082	−60	848	−22
Military	221	238	8	316	33	429	36	391	−9
Other	55	155	182	192	24	84	−56	118	40
Subtotal	$5,834	$13,349	129	$6,167	−54	$1,595	−74	$1,357	−15
• *Loans*									
Other	$144	$111	−23	$98	−12	$467	377	$381	−18
III. *Total Federal Student Aid*									
• *Available Funds*									
Grants	$ 6,292	$16,192	157	$10,615	−34	$ 6,673	−37	$ 7,028	5
Work	780	725	−7	1,039	43	822	−21	712	−13
Loans	4,451	4,354	−2	10,945	151	12,421	13	14,393	16
Subtotal	$11,523	$21,271	85	$22,599	6	$19,916	−12	$22,133	11
• *Composition of Funds*									
Grants	55%	76%		47%		34%		32%	
Work	7%	3%		5%		4%		3%	
Loans	39%	20%		48%		62%		65%	

Source: Calculated from College Board 1992.

grants, but by FY 1976, the amount of grant aid awarded had increased substantially while the loan aid had decreased slightly. Both grant and loan dollars awarded increased in the late 1970s, although loans grew more rapidly. In the 1980s, Title IV grant and loan programs increased at more moderate rates. Title IV aid grew modestly, despite moderate budget deficits.

When, however, these trends are examined from the perspective of specially directed programs (part II of the table), most of which existed before HEA, a different story emerges. Funding for specially directed programs increased substantially in the early 1970s—when funding for Title IV grant programs also expanded—then declined substantially in subsequent years. When specially directed programs are also considered, it is apparent that the modest growth in Title IV programs during the 1980s was more than offset by reductions in these specially directed programs.

Finally, when these trends are examined from the perspective of total funds made available to students through federal student aid programs (part III of the table), a more complete view of changes in federal student aid programs emerges. The total amount of student aid available increased in the early 1970s but remained stable thereafter. Moreover, the total amount of grant aid dropped substantially between FY 1976 and FY 1990, while the total amount of loan aid increased substantially. It should also be noted, however, that grant dollars increased slightly in the late 1980s, the result of a 10 percent increase in Pell grants.

The effects on student choice behavior
The research assessing the effects of federal student aid is examined from three vantages: trends in participation rates in relation to recent trends in funding for Title IV programs; the link between student aid and student enrollments; and enrollments of minority students.

Participation rates. One indicator commonly used as a measure of the effectiveness of Title IV programs is participation rates by ethnic groups. Trends in participation by race/ethnic group (see table 3) clearly indicate that participation rates for African-Americans declined beginning in the late 1970s through 1983 and rose after that. Participation rates for Hispanics declined in the middle 1980s, then climbed until 1989.

TABLE 3

TRENDS IN THE PERCENTAGE OF HIGH SCHOOL GRADUATES ENROLLED IN COLLEGE, BY RACE/ ETHNIC GROUP (1974-1990)

Year	White	African-American	Hispanic	Other
1974	48.7	40.5	53.1	69.3
1975	49.1	44.5	52.7	67.7
1976	50.3	45.3	53.6	57.3
1977	50.1	46.8	48.8	61.1
1978	50.4	47.5	46.1	56.4
1979	50.1	45.2	46.3	60.5
1980	51.5	44.0	49.6	64.3
1981	52.4	40.3	48.7	72.7
1982	54.2	38.8	49.4	69.0
1983	55.5	38.0	46.7	60.9
1984	57.9	39.9	49.3	60.1
1985	58.6	39.5	46.1	66.2
1986	58.5	43.5	42.3	72.5
1987	58.8	44.2	45.0	73.4
1988	60.1	49.7	48.5	73.9
1989	61.6	48.0	52.7	72.6
1990	63.0	48.9	52.5	72.6

Note: Because of the small sample sizes for "African-American," "Hispanic," and "Other," three-year averages were calculated. The three-year average for 1990 is the average percentage enrolling in college in 1989, 1990, and 1991. "Other" includes individuals who were not Hispanic, white, or African-American. Most were Asian and some were Native Americans.

Source: Alsalam et al. 1993. Calculated from Current Population Surveys, collected by the U.S. Bureau of the Census.

In contrast, participation rates for whites increased virtually every year throughout the entire period. What explains these swings in the participation rates of minorities? Could it be related to the changes in funding for federal student aid? The answers to these questions are actually quite complex, as they involve a judgment about causality.

Minority enrollments. After the decline in participation rates of minority students surfaced as a policy issue in the mid-1980s, policy analysts began to focus on the issue and its potential causes by drawing a possible link between the national downturn and the drop in federal grants (see, e.g., Wilson 1986). St_____ _to began to investigate the causes of _____ 37). In response to these concerns, _____ initiated a series of studies aimed at _____ ations for the downturn in participa-

_____ idy by a Department of Education con- _____ array of national data bases to examine _____ s and participation rates of minorities _____ ience of student aid. The use of enroll- _____ deemphasize the seriousness of the prob- _____ ity enrollments were climbing rather than _____ rcentage of the college-age population that was minority was also increasing. Specifically, the use of HEGIS (Higher Education General Information Survey) data allowed the research to emphasize that enrollment of African-Americans had actually increased between 1976 and 1984 (Chaikind ca. 1987). The report did not consider the effects of changes in pricing. Rather, it focused on factors outside the control of higher education:

> To understand the differences in black and white enroll-
> ment, . . . it is important to look beyond the observed enroll-
> ment figures. The evidence indicates that (1) many factors
> influence both black and white enrollment in institutions
> of higher education; and (2) most of these factors, such
> as academic achievement in elementary and secondary
> schools and family income, are largely beyond the control
> of the colleges (Chaikind ca. 1987, pp. 1–2).

The second report, a more comprehensive study that built on these basic principles, considered enrollments as well as participation rates and focused on factors outside the control of higher education (Pelavin and Kane 1988). The authors developed a more detailed analysis of the influence of academic preparation and included information on exemplary outreach programs aimed at improving minority students' preparation. The report gave an overview of federal programs but ignored the possibility that changes in federal student aid could have influenced the participation rates of minority students. Thus, this study, like the earlier one, focused on factors outside the control or influence of higher education institutions and agencies. Even the follow-up study ignored the effects of changes in prices and price subsidies (Pelavin and Kane 1990).

Student choice behavior. While the policy analysts who worked in the Department of Education ignored the influence of student aid on student enrollments, other recent studies firmly establish a link between student aid and enrollment (see, e.g., Leslie and Brinkman 1987, 1988; McPherson and Schapiro 1991; Paulsen 1990; St. John 1990a). Indeed, a substantial body of research indicates that student aid influences both first-time enrollments (Jackson 1978; Manski and Wise 1983; Paulsen 1990) and persistence (Astin 1975; Leslie and Brinkman 1988; St. John 1990b; St. John, Kirshstein, and Noell 1991; Terkla 1985). Thus, the decision to ignore the effects of student aid on the participation rates of minorities was a political one, influenced by the neoconservative belief that student aid was ineffectual.

A few studies that provide insight into the ways changes in student aid policy have combined to influence the participation of minority students merit consideration, given the lingering doubts about the effectiveness of student aid. First, an assessment of how the types of student aid packages that were being offered influenced enrollment, using the National Longitudinal Study of the High School Class of 1980 and High School and Beyond (the high school classes of 1980 and 1982), found that the types of aid packages offered in all three periods were "effective" in promoting first-time enrollment (that is, they had significant and positive coefficients) (St. John and Noell 1989). The study helped to establish a direct link between student aid and enrollments. Second, another study of the influence of student aid packages on year-to-year persistence by college attenders in the high school classes of 1972, 1980, and 1982 (St. John 1989) found that the types of student aid packages students received were effective in promoting persistence. Both studies used comprehensive logistic regression models that controlled for the range of variables in addition to those that influence first-time enrollment.

These studies not only confirmed a link between student aid and enrollment (both first-time enrollment and persistence), but also found that the effects of student aid could change over time as a result of changes in policy. They created a basis for assessing the effects of changes in policy, such as the shift from grants to loans, on enrollments by students from different economic backgrounds. A subsequent set of studies examined the effects of prices. One found that in the early 1980s, low-income students were responsive to the amount of grant they received, but not to the amount of loan they received, while middle-income students were more responsive to loans than grants (St. John 1990a). Another found that students were also responsive to prices in their decisions regarding persistence (St. John 1990b). These studies more clearly indicated that the *amount* of aid students received, rather than the type, influenced their enrollment.

Based on these studies, an estimate of the effects of changes in prices during the 1980s on enrollments during this period found that the changes in federal policy during the early 1980s improved middle-income enrollments at all types of institutions, but changes in federal grant policy influenced a shift of low-income enrollments from four-year colleges to two-year colleges or out of the higher education system altogether (St. John 1993b). Although these negative effects were mitigated somewhat by increased use of other institutional resources for grants in private four-year colleges, these findings demonstrate that changes in federal policy in the late 1970s and early 1980s, especially the decreases in federal grant dollars, influenced the decline in the participation rates of minorities.

The Federal Role in Promoting Productivity

In the middle 1980s, the U.S. Department of Education began to examine underlying issues related to productivity in higher education, in effect shifting the focus of the controversy about college costs from the effects of reductions in federal student aid to apparent inefficiencies in colleges and universities. Those studies focused attention on historical problems with "efficiency" in higher education and created a federal role in promoting productivity. This attack on higher education was consistent with the previous approach of investigating waste in federal programs, including student aid.

In the early 1980s, the federal government focused on waste, fraud, and abuse in the federal student aid programs. This emphasis was consonant with the initial Reagan mandate to reduce the costs of, and waste in, social programs. The initial quality control studies (e.g., Advanced Technology 1983, 1987) documented the costs to the federal government and proposed "corrective actions" for reducing this waste. A similar investigative approach was used to initiate the federal in-

quiries into ways of documenting waste and abuse in colleges
and universities, then developing plans to eliminate the waste.

The productivity of federal programs

The question of productivity in the federal student aid programs can be viewed from at least two vantages. One is technical and relates to efficiency in delivery, the other to the
effectiveness of various forms of student aid.

The first approach has been vigorously pursued in the past
15 years. During this period, the federal government has made
numerous technical improvements in the delivery of its Title
IV programs. A series of quality control studies measures the
sources and estimates the amounts of total error in the delivery of these programs (e.g., Advanced Technology 1983, 1987;
Wilson 1987). A number of technical improvements in the
delivery of student financial aid, such as the increased use
of validation of aid applications with parental and personal
tax forms, have been implemented as a result of these studies,
and such practices have generally improved the technical pro-
ficiency of the delivery of student aid. Many issues relative
to the efficiency of the delivery system remain, however, and
are periodically debated (e.g., Zook 1994b). While the aim
of the quality control studies—ensuring the technical efficiency of the federal student aid programs—is important to
taxpayers and the academic community because it can reduce
delivery costs of programs, the more critical questions relate
to whether federal financial aid strategies are cost-efficient
in promoting students' enrollment behavior.

A second approach involves thinking more critically about
how the federal role might evolve to promote better use of
resources in financing higher education. In the 1970s, it was
widely believed that grants were the most effective federal
strategy for promoting equal opportunity (Astin 1975; National
Commission on the Financing 1973). In the early 1980s, however, as more researchers began to investigate the effects of
loans, some claimed that loans were a more cost-efficient
means of promoting access (Tierney 1980a, 1980b). The
Department of Education began to sponsor policy research
emphasizing the effectiveness of loans (see, e.g., St. John and
Noell 1988). These early attempts to examine the effectiveness
of student loans were used to argue that loans were more
effective than grants rather than to assess when loans were
more cost-effective than grants and to design strategies that

optimize those effects. While it is now technically possible to craft a policy that builds on the strengths of grants and loans, given the current state of research on the effects of student financial aid, such an approach has not been attempted largely because of the ideological battles that permeate student aid policy. Nevertheless, it might be possible for the federal government to achieve more optimal returns from its own current investment in (level of expenditures on) student aid.

Promoting institutional productivity
In the past decade, the U.S. Department of Education has initiated a new wave of studies promoting institutional efficiency. While some of these efforts have simply taken the form of criticisms by public officials about the lack of institutional productivity, others advocate centralized cost-management strategies (see, e.g., U.S. Dept. of Education ca. 1990). These publications by the department can be viewed from a number of vantages.

If one accepts the tenets of the neoconservatives, the publication of *Tough Choices* (U.S. Dept. of Education ca. 1990) can be viewed as a constructive step, aimed at putting new tools in the hands of college and university administrators. The text promotes the systematic study of college costs as a means of achieving several goals:

> *There are ways to reduce staff, minimize the human pain that staff reduction can involve, and improve services at the same time. These ways can be identified through a cost-management study* (U.S. Dept. of Education ca. 1990, p. 4).

Thus, the booklet can be viewed as an attempt to address explicitly problems that institutions themselves have been unable to address.

When this document is viewed more critically, however, it becomes evident that the department produced a document that promotes adaptive strategic planning, an approach that has not been widely adopted in higher education (Chaffee 1985). Indeed, the department's document proclaims the cost management study as a comprehensive process that embraces all aspects of institutional life:

> *A cost management study must not be a short-term, narrowly focused project. Rather, it should be an exhaustive*

process of assessing the quality and cost of an institution's support services, identifying opportunities for improvement and enrichment. It focuses on all the functions that support a university's teaching, research, and community service objectives, and recommends ways in which these functions [can] be performed better, at less cost, or both (U.S. Dept. of Education ca. 1990, p. 4).

This passage communicates the assumptions that seem to guide recent federal efforts to promote cost reduction in higher education: that inefficiency is pervasive in higher education; that exhaustive study can identify ways that services can be improved; and that the full range of services universities provide—including teaching, research, and community service—can somehow be performed more efficiently, at reduced cost and improved quality. Implicit in these claims is a belief that centralized strategic action can achieve two goals that are difficult to reconcile in higher education—improving quality and reducing operating costs.

This latter claim becomes more problematic, at least from the faculty's perspective, when the past 15 years of administrative action in higher education is considered, a period during which emphasis on centralized strategic action has increased (Chaffee 1984, 1985, 1989; Keller 1983; Norris and Poulton 1987; Steeples 1988b). These developments, which arise from premises similar to those evident in *Tough Choices* (U.S. Dept. of Education ca. 1990), ironically might have contributed more to the rise in administrative costs than any other single factor. It thus appears that the federal government is promoting strategies that could raise, rather than reduce, administrative costs. Indeed, the issue of how college costs can most effectively be dealt with is a more complex issue than recognized in federal reports promoting cost management.

Recently, the Clinton administration's plan to require regional accrediting associations to monitor default rates (Leatherman 1994), which is an attempt to use regulation to promote what is perceived to be more efficient behavior, seems especially counterproductive for two reasons: (1) default rates seem more related to a student's background than to institutional practices regarding loans (Wilms, Moore, and Bolus 1987), meaning that high default rates are influenced by the increased emphasis on loans; and (2) accrediting associations are currently a force that inhibit, rather than promote, productivity as a result of their emphasis on maintaining high production functions (low student/faculty ratios and class sizes). Thus, the Clinton administration's attempts to regulate accreditation to penalize institutions with high default rates not only perpetuate neoconservative assumptions about higher education finance, but also could further reduce access.

Federal Student Aid as an Investment

The return on the public's investment in student financial aid can be thought of in at least two ways. The more common, more frequently advocated approach is to relate gains in productivity to the public investment in education (Kramer 1993a). An alternative is to estimate the amount of tax revenue returns attributable to the public investment, an approach that has only recently been used.

The links between the state of the national economy and the public investment in education are exceedingly difficult to determine. While the claim that public spending on higher education might have contributed to the recession in the late 1980s (Hansen 1983) has been proven false (McPherson and Schapiro 1991), it illustrates the difficulty economists and policy analysts have in interpreting the link between higher education funding and the state of the economy. Clearly, the link between economic conditions and student aid is difficult to assess when conventional means are used (Kramer 1993a).

An alternative approach to assessing returns on the government's investment is to assess the direct tax revenues gained from public expenditures on higher education. Recent research indicates that individual returns from higher education are substantial (Alexander 1976; Leslie 1990; Leslie and Brinkman 1986, 1988; Pascarella and Terenzini 1991), even for minorities (Pascarella, Smart, and Stoecker 1989), and further that they started to grow again in the middle 1970s (Institute for Research 1994; O'Neill and Sepielli 1988) after a period of decline (Freeman 1976). Further, substantial returns accrue to both men and women for attending college and receiving a bachelor's degree or a graduate degree (although the returns to women do not mitigate the basic inequities in earnings between men and women) (Leslie and Brinkman 1986, 1988; Pascarella, Smart, and Stoecker 1989). The decline in returns observed in prior decades (Freeman 1976) apparently has been reversed.

The links between the state of the national economy and the public investment in education are exceedingly difficult to determine.

One recent study examines tax revenue returns on the federal investment in need-based financial aid programs, arguing that the costs and benefits of vocational and postsecondary programs can be assessed using tax revenue returns derived from increases in educational attainment attributable to public expenditures (Levin 1983). Based on these arguments, another study assessed the influence student financial aid had on the educational attainment of students in the high school class of 1972, then estimated the future federal tax revenue returns attributable to those gains and the actual costs of the subsidies provided (St. John and Masten 1990). The study concluded that the tax revenue returns to the federal government were more than four times the costs, a ratio that does not take into account the *indirect* gains, such as reduced social welfare costs. While this line of inquiry indicates that federal returns on its investment in student aid are substantial, the methods of estimation used in these studies can no doubt be refined.

Assessing Ideological Claims

This review of research provides evidence relating to the five ideological claims. First, the conservative claim was directly relevant to the review of the federal role in student financial aid. Consistent with the conventional conservative position, considerable returns accrue to individual investment in higher education, which appear to have improved in the past two decades.

Second, the conventional liberal claims about the public investment in higher education seem problematic when critically examined. It is difficult to prove a causal link between spending on student aid and the state of the national economy. It could also be illogical to claim that such a criterion should be used as a basis for public spending, as many other factors in addition to student aid influence the state of the economy.

Further, the argument that student aid provides intergenerational equity is also quite problematic. While recent research seems to have clarified that a link exists between prices (and price subsidies) and the opportunity of low- and middle-income students (and prospective students) to attend college, this general criterion provides only a limited basis for making refined judgments about what levels or types of spending are necessary or appropriate. When is the public investment sufficient to achieve intergenerational equity? This weakness of the conventional liberal argument could be exploited, even if no lingering doubts existed about the effectiveness of student aid.

Third, two of the neoconservative arguments about higher education finance were germane to the analysis of the effects of changes in the federal role. The neoconservative claim that student aid has no effect on equal opportunity is the logical basis for most of the other neoconservative criticisms about higher education finance, but it is not substantiated by the evidence. Specifically, the research indicates that student aid has a marked influence on student choice behavior.

The neoconservative claim that poor academic achievement rather than student aid explains the decline in the participation rates of minorities also appears ill founded. The research on the effects of student aid demonstrates that a link exists between the types and amounts of aid minority students received and their enrollment. Further, in the late 1980s and early 1990s, when the federal government again placed more emphasis on grants for low-income students, African-American enrollments began to climb again.

Fourth, the reconstructed neoliberal claim that tax revenue returns provide a possible basis for making funding decisions is at least partially supported. One study found that federal student aid results in a substantial tax revenue return to the federal government. Even if this phenomenon were substantiated by subsequent studies, however, it does not necessarily provide sufficient rationale to argue for more aid. Even though federal student aid has only a "marginal" influence on first-time college attendance and persistence, the gains in educational attainment attributable to these expenditures are substantial. Indeed, the high rate of return seems sufficient to justify the practice of using tax revenues to support students. The argument that the federal investment should be increased just because the return is high has its limitations, however. It is possible, for example, that increased federal expenditures would reduce the rate of return unless gains in productivity occurred.

Finally, the neo-Marxist argument that minority students were negatively influenced by cuts in federal grants was substantiated. Indeed, an apparent deception is embedded in the Reagan administration's claim that student aid was not effective and its subsequent denial that changes in policy could have influenced the downturn in the participation rates of African-Americans.

STATE FINANCING STRATEGIES

Historically, states have funded institutions through direct appropriations, which subsidized educational costs and kept tuition low. If appropriations drop and educational costs remain stable, then prices usually increase (Atwell and Hauptman 1986; Frances 1985; Hines 1988; Layzell and Lyddon 1990). States also support need- and merit-based grant programs, although the extent of these programs varies substantially across states. And funding for institutions and grant programs is seldom coordinated in a way that would mitigate the effects of increased tuition on public institutions (Griswold and Marine *In press*). Unfortunately, both types of funding usually rise and fall together (Griswold and Marine *In press;* Hines 1988). This section examines research on the states' evolving role in the pricing process (institutional and student subsidies), the states' potential role in promoting productivity in higher education, and the viability of viewing the states' financial role through the emerging investment lens. Finally, it reflects on whether the research supports the various ideological claims emerging from the controversy over college costs.

The States' Role in Pricing

Because of their role in funding institutions and students, states' decisions directly influence both prices—especially the amount public institutions charge—and students' ability to pay for college through student grant programs. State strategies are seldom coordinated in a way that would maintain access, especially at times when tax revenues are declining, although such strategies are possible if states increase grants when they decrease appropriations (Hearn and Anderson 1989; Hearn and Longanecker 1985; St. John 1991a).

Most criticism of states in the 1980s focused on the influence of decreases in appropriations on increases in prices. For example, "cost containment alone is not the answer because increasing costs are not the sole problem" (Eiser 1988, p. 18). Further:

> The major cause for rising tuitions is shortfalls in revenues from public sources. . . . *When revenues from public sources dwindle, tuitions are raised to make up the difference. As a result, more of the costs have been shifted to the student and families through higher tuition* (Eiser 1988, p. 18, emphasis in original).

This criticism of states, one frequently made in the literature on higher education finance in the 1980s (Hines 1988), focuses exclusively on the link between institutional subsidies and prices. The shift in the burden for financing public higher education from states to students and their families, a consequence of the decline in state support, was increasingly an issue of concern to national groups examining responsibilities for financing higher education (Hauptman 1993; Kramer 1993b).

Unfortunately, the link between shifts in state support of institutions and their role in financing state grant programs is seldom even acknowledged. Instead, states have generally maintained a position that their decisions have not influenced access. For example, according to one study of college costs:

In most states, enrollments have grown as record increases in tuition were imposed. While the research is not definitive, higher education does not seem to be a price-sensitive industry. Still, different segments of the population probably respond differently and states need to become more explicit in their desires to maintain access and improve the quality of undergraduate and graduate programs. There are indications that participation by minorities and low-income students [could] be adversely influenced by the perceived cost of going to college even if net price is substantially lower because of financial aid. On the other hand, the decline in minority enrollment seems to track the shift in federal aid from grants to loans, indicating that net price is very much the issue (State Higher Education 1988, p. 7).

This statement provides an insight into the perspective of state executive officers on the link between prices and enrollments. Because enrollments climbed at a time when net prices rose, observers assumed that students and prospective students were not price sensitive. It also acknowledges that the downturn in minority enrollment, a big political issue in the 1980s (Chaikind ca. 1987; Mingle 1987; Pelavin and Kane 1988), might be linked to changes in federal grant policy; however, it virtually ignores the possibility that this problem could be an unintended consequence of changes in states' financing policies. Thus, the policy literature on higher education focuses on the link between state appropriations and tuition but minimizes the possibility that reductions in state grants could also be problematic or that a simultaneous increase in prices in the public sector and reduction in state student grants could limit access. Rather, states attribute responsibility for equal opportunity to the federal government.

States and pricing

While the link between reduced state funding and rising prices in public colleges and universities has been widely discussed in the research literature (Hauptman 1990a, 1990b; Hauptman and Hartle 1987; Kirshstein, Tikoff, et al. 1990), most of the literature focuses on trends in the early 1980s, and it is important to consider whether these trends have continued. Trends in state support for grant programs also merit explicit consideration.

Appropriations to institutions. One observer notes:

In some states, worsening economic conditions [might] require reduction in support of higher education, and when that case occurs, institutions rely more on revenue from student tuition. . . . While none of these financing devices can substitute for a base budget, their contribution to an institution's overall financial health can make the difference between a moderately optimistic picture and a fiscally bleak one (Hines 1988, p. 53).

These observations seemed to foreshadow the developments during the next few years. In the early 1980s, support had wavered in some states but overall grew marginally. In the late 1980s—and especially in the early 1990s—however, states' subsidies to public colleges and universities wavered further. In the early 1990s, reductions were widespread:

State support for higher education in the 1993 fiscal year showed a distinctly negative pattern for the second year in a row. One year ago, for the first time on record, state governments appropriated less to higher education than in the preceding year. But in 1992, state governments had appropriated less to higher education for FY1993 than in either FY92 or FY91, effectively turning back the total

amount appropriated nationally to the FY90 level
(Hines 1993, p. 1).

Further complicating this overall pattern is the fact that most
states have not increased their support of state grant programs
enough to mitigate the increases in tuition associated with
these reductions in institutional support. Between 1990 and
1991, 12 states reduced their support for state grant programs
(seven by 10 percent or more), five had less than 1 percent
change, and 13 increased grants by 1 to 4 percent (Davis, Nastelli, and Redd 1993). Thus, in more than half the states, expenditures for grants did not even keep pace with inflation.
Further, most states simultaneously increase or decrease both
their institutional and student subsidies, and, given that institutions generally raise tuitions when their government subsidies are reduced, the process of simultaneously reducing
institutional and student aid could contribute to problems
with enrollments.

Pricing in the public sector. The link between state appropriations and tuition is most easily explained in relation to
educational costs (average expenditures per student). Institutions tend to maintain their costs when appropriations drop
by increasing tuition sufficiently to mitigate the loss in appropriations. Most states (32 of 48 responding to one survey)
use this mechanism: "Tuition is set in the historical pattern—
to generate all or most of the difference between what the
institutions believed they needed and what state governments
appropriated" (Curry 1988, p. 6). All of the other states in the
survey used some type of formula model, "an approach where
statutes, rules, or budget procedures predict or set tuition rates
or assumed revenues from tuition" (p. 6). The extent to which
the formula used in these states explicitly considers state
appropriations when setting tuition varies substantially. In
some states, the formula essentially adjusts tuition charges
to budget requirements; in others the link is not evident
(Curry 1988). Even in states where the formula would seem
to preclude institutions' raising tuition charges to adjust to
decreases in appropriations, however, the adjustments are
made when necessary. For example, in the past few years in
California, a state with a "formula" that precludes setting tuition based on budget requirements, education fees were
raised substantially when state appropriations declined in the

past few years (Griswold and Marine *In press;* Knutsen 1993; Mingle 1988b; St. John 1993a).

Most recent studies of the relationship between state appropriations and educational expenditures focus on the early 1980s. These analyses indicate not only a transfer in responsibility for financing public institutions from states to students, but also modest growth in educational expenditures (Kirshstein, Tikoff, et al. 1990; St. John 1992a). Table 4 presents an analysis of the relationship between education and related expenditures and revenues from state appropriations and tuition. The ratio of revenue from state appropriations and tuition to educational expenditures dropped by about 7 percentage points between 1985–86 and 1990–91, from 69.6 percent to 62.5 percent. Further, the percentage of education expenditures covered by tuition increased by about 4 percentage points, from 23.4 percent to 26.6 percent. Thus, the trends observed in the early 1980s continued in the late 1980s. Two caveats must be considered, however: Appropriations dollars were not directly replaced dollar for dollar with tuition dollars; and public institutions used other revenue sources, in addition to tuition, to support educational expenditures. Nevertheless, there should be little doubt that public colleges and universities do, in general, substitute for the loss of state appropriations by raising tuition charges, even if it is not dollar for dollar, and that the means states use to finance public colleges and universities during the past decade have been restructured.

Because states vary substantially in their governance structures (Hearn and Griswold 1994; Hines 1988; Volkwein 1987, 1989), it is natural to inquire about the influence of governance on financial strategies. It has been found that strong centralization and coordination are not related to the quality of a university (Volkwein 1989), although another well-designed study found that strong state centralization—having a strong coordinating board or a single state governing board—increased the probability of educational innovations (Hearn and Griswold 1994). The juxtaposition of these findings suggests that mandating educational innovations, such as the use of student assessments, has little measurable influence on quality. Further, neither strong coordination nor centralized governing boards were associated with innovative financing strategies, such as creating educational savings plans (Hearn and Griswold 1994). "Unlike educational innovations,

TABLE 4

**RECENT CHANGES IN EDUCATIONAL EXPENDITURES
AND REVENUES FOR STATE APPROPRIATIONS IN
PUBLIC INSTITUTIONS (Millions of Dollars)**

	1985-86	1990-91
Education and Related Expenditures	$40,340	$57,390
Revenue from State Appropriations	$28,071	$35,899
Tuition Revenue	$9,439	$15,258
Ratio of State Appropriations to Education Expenditures	.6959	.6255
Ratio of Tuition Revenue to Education Expenditures	.2340	.2659

Note: "Education and related expenditures" is the sum of expenditures on instruction, administration (academic support minus libraries, institutional support, and student services), libraries, and plant operations and maintenance.

Source: Calculated from information in Snyder 1993.

which may be seen as essentially regulatory in nature, actions to aid in financing postsecondary attendance are unquestionably redistributive in intent and thus subject to a more diffuse set of influences" (p. 183).

More generally, periods of oscillating levels of state support for public institutions appear related to economic conditions (Froomkin 1990; Hauptman 1992), as state appropriations for student aid and to institutions tend to vary according to the availability of tax revenues (Hines 1988, 1993). Few states even attempt to coordinate tuition and student aid (Layzell and Lyddon 1990). A recent examination of efforts to coordinate tuition and aid strategies in five states that had attempted coordination found that only one of those states, Minnesota, had successfully linked tuition and grants in a high-tuition, high-aid strategy (Griswold and Marine *In press*). The other states allowed tuitions to rise without adjusting student grants. Thus, variations in state governance appear inconsequential in analyses of the effects of state financing strategies on enrollment, although their relationship certainly merits further investigation.

The effects of changes in state pricing policy
If one assumes that students do not respond to prices (State Higher Education 1988), then it is also logical to conclude that shifting the burden for financing public higher education

from states to students and their families has no effect on access. Recent empirical studies, however, indicate this assumption is not true (McPherson and Schapiro 1991; St. John 1991b). A review of the conclusions of recent studies makes it possible to discern the effects of changes in prices on student choice behavior.

First-time enrollment. One way to assess whether students' decisions about whether to enroll in college (access) and the types of institutions they actually attend (choice of school) were influenced by the restructuring of state finance policy is to examine the effect of aid on first-time enrollments. Such generic types of enrollment decisions, characterized here as "first-time enrollment decisions," can be influenced by changes in prices. A series of recent studies indicates that rising prices across the board in higher education had the effect of forcing middle- and lower-income students toward less expensive institutions or out of higher education altogether. One study found that changes in prices influenced low-income students in the 1980s to enroll in less expensive colleges and universities (Pascarella, Smart, and Smylie 1992). Another study of the influence of prices and price subsidies on first-time enrollment decisions by students in the high school class of 1982 found that low-income students were more responsive to grants than to tuition but were not responsive to loans, while middle-income students were more responsive to loans than to grants and more responsive to grants than to tuition (St. John 1990a). A third study used the delta-p statistics for tuition and price subsidies (grants and loans) developed in the second study to estimate the effects of actual changes in tuition and student aid in the early 1980s on the pattern of enrollment (St. John 1993b). It concluded that state policy changes in the early 1980s—especially the fact that tuition increased faster in four-year colleges—influenced a redistribution of low-income enrollment from public four-year to public two-year colleges.

In combination, the findings of these studies seem to suggest that continuing the current approach to financial restructuring in most states—and simultaneously reducing state appropriations to institutions and student grant programs—has had a detrimental effect on enrollments of low-income students. In fall 1993, this problem apparently became more visible as many states encountered just such a severe enroll-

Rising prices forced middle- and lower-income students toward less expensive institutions or out of higher education altogether.

ment decline. Twelve of 14 states responding to a survey by the American Council on Education indicated a decline in fall enrollments, which was "believed caused by reduced course offerings, tuition increases, and enrollment ceilings associated with state budget constraints and increased job opportunities accompanying the economic recovery" (Associated Press 1993). The largest drops recorded in the survey, 9 percent, were in the California community colleges, where the declines were attributed to reductions in course offerings and price increases (Freedberg 1993, p. A16).

Persistence. A series of recent national studies has examined the influence of prices and price subsidies on persistence.[2] A few merit mention, particularly those providing evidence that recent changes in state financing strategies are decreasing opportunities for continuous enrollment and increasing the length of time it takes students to attain their degrees.[3] The first, using the National Postsecondary Student Aid Survey of 1986–87 (NPSAS-87), separately examined the effects of prices and price subsides on within-year persistence (the reenrollment in the spring semester after being enrolled in the fall) by traditional-age undergraduate students in public and private four-year colleges (St. John, Oescher, and Andrieu 1992). It found that in private colleges tuition was negatively associated with persistence, while grants were positively associated with persistence. In contrast, in public colleges, both tuition and grants were negatively associated with persistence, and tuition had a much larger negative association with persistence in public colleges than in private colleges. The authors concluded that private four-year colleges were in a more competitive position than public four-year colleges.

2. An extensive body of institutional studies of persistence uses models developed by Tinto (1975, 1987) and Bean (1980, 1982; Bean and Metzner 1985). Both models consider the effects of academic and social integration on decisions affecting persistence (Cabrera et al. 1992). Most of these studies (e.g., Bean 1985; Pascarella and Terenzini 1979, 1980, 1988, 1991) do not explicitly consider the effects of student aid, but reviews of the literature on persistence that does consider the effects of student aid consistently confirm that a relationship exists (Leslie and Brinkman 1988).

3. See Cabrera, Stampen, and Hansen (1990), St. John, Kirshstein, and Noell (1991), and St. John, et al. (1994) for discussions of the relationships between the social and academic integration concepts developed by Tinto (1975) and Bean (1980) and the types of data elements available in national data bases.

Second, a series of recent persistence studies using NPSAS-87 found that students enrolled in public colleges were less likely to persist than students enrolled in private colleges. The studies examined traditional-age undergraduates enrolled in four-year colleges (St. John, et al. 1994), traditional-age students enrolled in two-year colleges (St. John and Starkey 1994), non-traditional-age undergraduates enrolled in four-year colleges (Tynes 1993), and graduate students (Andrieu and St. John 1993). The studies consistently found that students in public colleges and universities are less likely to persist, at least when prices were considered. Further, analyses that separately examine students enrolled in public and private colleges suggest that differences in the set of prices students face are a partial explanation for why public college students persist at lower rates (Andrieu and St. John 1993; St. John, et al. 1994; St. John, Oescher, and Andrieu 1992). While tuition is still lower in public colleges, students who attend public colleges are more price sensitive.

Low-income and minority enrollment. Like the national studies on enrollment of minority students (Chaikind ca. 1987; Pelavin and Kane 1988) discussed earlier, the SHEEO (State Higher Education Executive Officers) study on minority enrollment considered enrollment levels as well as participation rates and focused on academic preparation as the primary cause of the downturn (Mingle 1987). This research, like the other SHEEO documents discussed above, deemphasized the fact that changes in state policy (such as the increase in tuition in public institutions) could be a source of the problem. Other research about higher education finance, however, indicates that state policies as well as federal policy influenced the decline in minority participation rates.

The recent studies of persistence using NPSAS-87 indicate that, in the late 1980s, prices had a negative influence on persistence by African-Americans. An analysis of traditional-age students in four-year colleges found that, while African-Americans were more likely than others to persist in private four-year colleges, they were less likely to persist in public four-year colleges (St. John, Oescher, and Andrieu 1992). Analysis of traditional college-age students enrolled in public two-year colleges found that African-Americans were more likely to persist. These findings further indicate that the pricing policies of states in the 1980s essentially influenced the de facto segregation of African-Americans in higher education by encouraging their enrollment in two-year colleges and *dis*-couraging their enrollment in public four-year colleges.

Thus, the pricing mechanisms currently being used by states have a different effect on African-Americans and whites. African-Americans are substantially more sensitive to tuition charges. In particular, the annual tuition increases by public four-year institutions have incrementally diminished post-secondary opportunities for African-American students. These developments appear to be a direct result of the incremental budget process used by many states in cutting appropriations to institutions and student grant programs when tax dollars are short.

An alternative approach

An alternative approach to states' role in financing higher edu-cation—linking increases in need-based student grants to reductions in state appropriations to institutions (and tuition increases)—has been widely advocated (Hearn and Longa-necker 1985; McPherson and Schapiro 1991; Wallace 1992) but not widely used. The research to date indicates that this approach potentially can overcome the limitations of the cur-rent practices although it might be limited in the extent to which the high-tuition, high-aid strategy can remedy the problem.

Minnesota has experimented with the use of a high-tuition, high-aid strategy. In the early 1980s, a number of theories developed by scholars of higher education in Minnesota created an environment conducive to bold new action, includ-ing an argument that the high-tuition, high-aid strategy could be a more equitable basis for the state's funding of higher education (Hearn and Longanecker 1985) and a logical basis for cost-centered tuition, which had been experimented with at the University of Minnesota (Berg and Hoenack 1987).

In 1984, the state of Minnesota adopted a financing policy that included raising the portion of costs subsidized by tuition revenue to one-third and increasing the level of need-based grants to promote access. Initial evaluations of this experiment indicated that it maintained access, improved the overall fund-ing level for public colleges and universities, and maintained minority enrollment (Hearn and Anderson 1989; St. John 1991a). Thus, initial indications are that the high-tuition, high-aid strategy can overcome some of the deficiencies associated with the more common practice of ignoring the link between tuition and aid.

Additionally, when the high-tuition, high-aid strategy is used in public four-year institutions, at least some potential exists to gain additional revenues from the Pell grant program as tuitions rise, as the public institutions in Minnesota did when the new tuition policy was implemented (Hearn and Anderson 1989). Further, an econometric analysis found that "public four-year institutions tend to raise tuition by $450 for every $100 increase in federal student aid" (McPherson and Schapiro 1991, p. 72), indicating that public institutions derive some benefit from raising tuitions in the form of federal grant revenue.

The high-tuition, high-aid strategy has some possible limitations, however. The strategy could be having a detrimental effect on the academic progress of students in state colleges and community colleges in Minnesota (Lopez 1993), and the provision to cover 50 percent of costs in the state grant program could limit access in Minnesota, given the high cost of attending (Griswold and Marine *In press*). Further, a recent state evaluation found that some Pell recipients (the poorest students) received no state grants, while some students from families earning over $100,000 received state grants (Jackson-Beeck et al. 1994). These recent studies suggest that, at a minimum, the provision to cover 50 percent of costs in the Minnesota grant program should be reconsidered. Perhaps grant aid should cover 60 percent or more of costs for needy students when the cost of attending high-cost public institutions is being considered. A more recent analysis reveals that, without the state grant program, the high-tuition strategy in Minnesota would be "regressive," with low-income families paying more after Pell awards and expected contributions than middle- and upper-income students (Minnesota Higher Education 1994). Even exemplary state programs merit periodic reanalysis.

The States' Role in Promoting Productivity
The emerging issue of productivity in higher education presents a particularly perplexing problem for states. Rather than focusing on productivity, states have generally focused on promoting "quality." This mission is ambiguous, however:

There is a general confusion about the relationship between the quality of education and its cost. This confusion is found within the higher education community. Because the capacity to document quality differences has not been developed, prestige seems to accrue to colleges and universities that charge more (State Higher Education 1988, p. 7).

A link appears to exist between high revenue and quality ratings. One study found that the quality ranking of public research universities was related to their level of funding (Volkwein 1989), and another found that "institutions [that] are relatively free of state controls are less dependent on state appropriations and raise a larger portion of their funds from nonstate sources" (Volkwein 1987, p. 145). More generally, "legislative frustration over the fixed nature of higher education costs and the failure of institutions to set priorities is also directed at the boards" (Mingle 1988a, p. 4). This general frustration over the role of states in promoting quality complicates, and possibly even limits, the ability of states to deal with issues of productivity. A few recent studies illustrate the types of actions states take to promote "productivity" and the consequences of those types of actions.

A poor record in cost management
States generally lack mechanisms for managing cost (Kramer 1993b; Mingle 1988a). The Minnesota case is one of the few recent successful examples of a governor, a legislature, and public systems of higher education developing a scheme for dealing with program costs in the framework of comprehensive state financing (Berg and Hoenack 1987; Hearn and Anderson 1989). In the absence of deliberate study of productivity and cost management issues in most states, the budget process has become a battleground in many states for reconciling the recent public concern about productivity in higher education with historical concerns about quality and the level of public funding.

The issue of productivity in public higher education has emerged as a political issue in many states in the 1990s. In California faculty workloads and growth in administrative costs have become critical issues in the battles over the budget, in Maine the legislature has requested cuts in administrators' salaries, and in Louisiana the legislature enacted a law creating a new state-level body to study means of promoting productivity (St. John 1993a). In many states, higher education is one of the few areas of the state budget that is not constitutionally protected from reductions (Hines 1988; St. John 1991a). These developments leave public higher education in a poor position to compete with other claimants for state tax dollars and have probably influenced higher education's facing reductions in state funding in the early 1990s (Hines 1993). Thus retrenchment, the process of making incremental cuts in university budgets, apparently is becoming the primary mechanism for states to "manage" costs.

Attempts to link funding to outcomes

The fact that some states have attempted to link assessment of student outcomes to their financing strategies (Hines 1988) further complicates the mechanisms used to finance public higher education. Twenty states have adopted statewide assessment techniques for public higher education (Hearn and Griswold 1994). While some methods of assessing student outcomes in higher education have been proven (Jacobi, Astin, and Ayala 1987; Pascarella and Terenzini 1991), it is extremely difficult to link specific student outcomes to institutional goals and actions (Jacobi, Astin, and Ayala 1987), further complicating attempts to use quality assessments in funding. Part of the problem is that it is extremely difficult to measure the value added by college (Pascarella and Terenzini 1991). It would therefore appear that the construction of funding strategies rewarding colleges and universities for the value they add is beyond the state of the art of educational measurement. Another part of the problem is that no evidence supports the contention that central control and mandated reforms influence learning outcomes positively. Quite the contrary, as research indicates a reverse relationship exists between centralization and quality for state universities (Volkwein 1989) and that states with strong coordination and centralized governance structures are more likely to have mandated outcomes assessment (Hearn and Griswold 1994), ample reason exists to be cautious about attempts to link the results of mandated assessments to state funding strategies.

The impact of retrenchment

Because of the history of institutional autonomy (Hines 1988; Mingle 1988a), institutions generally maintain discretion over how expenditures are reduced when states reduce their financial support. Research on the impact of retrenchment processes, although relatively recent, seems to point to some recurring themes. First, programs that serve the middle-class professions are the most frequently cut when institutions develop their retrenchment plans (Gumport 1993; Slaughter 1993a). Second, it also appears that this priority is consistent with the priorities embedded in institutional strategic plans. An analysis of retrenchment processes at two university campuses found not only that middle-class professions were hardest hit by budget reductions, but also that these priorities were consistent with the two universities' planning priorities (St. John 1993a). Further, many of the programs that were protected in the process had lower demand and higher costs than programs that were cut.

These developments raise questions about the convergence of institutional priorities and the broader social concerns about access and productivity. The middle-class professions, like education and nursing, often represent the types of majors that offer a way out of poverty and consequently are often in high demand. Yet when institutions are faced with choices about what to cut, they are more likely to cut these middle-class programs than those associated with elite professions and high prestige (Gumport 1993; Slaughter 1993a, 1993b).[4]

Public Higher Education as an Investment

The literature on higher education generally makes an association between earnings and state support for higher education, generally confirming the argument that education has high individual returns. The evidence of a link between spending on higher education and economic development, however, has generally been more difficult to document (Hines 1988; Kramer 1993a; Leslie and Brinkman 1988). The difficulty researchers have with documenting the link between state spending on higher education and its economic growth has added to the difficulty state boards and institutions have in making their case to state legislatures (Hines 1988).

Three recent studies have examined the link between state support of higher education and its tax revenue returns, from

---

4. One alternative hypothesis is that institutions cut programs because they have higher costs per credit hour, a possibility meriting investigation. Another alternative is that programs serving minority students are treated as "cash cows" (Kotler and Murphy 1981; Winston 1994) that are milked to support "rising stars" (programs that serve elite professions) when resources are available and cut to protect these programs when resources are scarce.

income tax and other sources, a method that has been advocated by some economists (e.g., Levin 1983). A study of the economic impact of the University of Massachusetts at Boston estimates the income to the state from its support of the university:

> *Hence,* for every $1 spent by the commonwealth on UMB students, it can expect to receive in return an added $1.57 in personal income and sales taxes. *Measuring this ratio in investment terms yields a rate of return to the state government of 8.9 percent—significantly more than the state could earn if it were allowed to invest in long-term U.S. Treasury Bonds, corporate bonds, or even the typical mutual fund* (Bluestone 1993, p. 2, emphasis in the original).

A second study of the economic impact of the state's investment in the California state university system found that the state could expect to receive about two dollars (net present value) in state tax revenue for every dollar it spent on the system (Girling, Goldman, and Keith 1993). And a third recent study, which examined the direct economic impact of Texas's appropriations to higher education by considering the effects of state appropriations on state income (tax revenues), payroll, and jobs found that "by calculating the ratio between . . . net state income (or gross state product) and . . . appropriations, the state received an additional $1.13 in economic activity for every dollar invested in the public higher education industry" (Creech, Carpenter, and Davis 1994, p. 134). Additionally, substantial gains were made in state payroll and jobs. Thus, even states with regressive tax structures apparently receive positive returns from their spending on public higher education.

An alternative method of assessing the economic impact of state investments in higher education is to assess the impact of state expenditures on productivity of the workforce, an approach that is compatible with the more conventional concepts of intergenerational equity and productivity (Becker 1964; Kramer 1993a, 1993b). One recent study examining the influence of changes in state spending on higher education on growth in productivity of the workforce from 1980 to 1989 (Paulsen 1994) concluded that "investment in higher education explains a substantial portion of the variation in workforce productivity among states" (p. 9).

Assessing Ideological Claims

First, the liberal claims about the value of taxpayers' invest-ment in higher education are supported by recent research but are more difficult to interpret and could be of little prac-tical use in the current debates about higher education finance. The possible exception to this conclusion is that a recent study found a positive association between state spend-ing on higher education and productivity of the workforce (Paulsen 1994). Regarding the argument about cross-genera-tional equity, the evidence is also difficult to interpret, but the evidence presented so far reinforces the conclusion that prices and price subsidies only marginally influence access (Leslie and Brinkman 1988; McPherson and Schapiro 1991).

The liberal claim that economic growth should provide the basis for public decisions to invest in education is even more problematic for state officials. The link between general eco-nomic measures and the taxpayers' investment in higher edu-cation is difficult to measure. Further, because numerous fac-tors other than higher education influence state economies, the concept of general economic return provides a prob-lematic basis for making decisions about state support for higher education. To the extent that proponents of higher education rely on the liberal ideology when they argue for public support of higher education, they would appear to be in a weak position, relative to conservative and neoconser-vative arguments.

Second, the analysis of the impact of changes in the state role support some of the neoconservative claims about higher education finance but not others. Contrary to neoconservative claims, the research clearly indicates that taxpayers' investment in student aid does have an impact on enrollment, and it is especially evident when the effects of the high-tuition, high-aid strategy used in Minnesota are compared to the effects on enrollment of the nationwide pattern of shifting the bur-den for supporting public institutions to students and their families. Thus, the neoconservative claim that student aid does not influence enrollment is not supported by the research on state finance.

The evidence on states, however, does support two of the neoconservative claims about higher education finance. The evidence indicates that public four-year institutions do gain additional revenues from student aid when they raise tuition (McPherson and Schapiro 1991). This tendency has cushioned the effect of higher tuition in public institutions (St. John 1993b), thus reinforcing some state officials' false belief that students are not responsive to prices (State Higher Education 1988). Specifically, middle-income students borrow more money when tuition increases, which raises the probability of their continued enrollment, while some low-income students are more likely to rely on Pell grants. These developments disguise the regressive effects of price increases by the public sector, which seems especially problematic, given the general pattern of financial restructuring now evident in many states. The process of financial restructuring appears to have a detrimental effect on enrollment of low-income and minority students in public four-year institutions (Kaltenbaugh 1993; Pascarella, Smart, and Smylie 1992; St. John 1993b).

Further, the neoconservative claim that colleges and universities are unproductive and wasteful appears especially problematic for states. The states' record in cost management seems poor. State agencies try to support institutional arguments that quality is related to the level of public support (Mingle 1988a; State Higher Education 1988), yet state regulations appear to impede quality and productivity (Volkwein 1987). States have not developed a viable approach to cost management in higher education, however, which has created tensions between legislatures and public institutions of higher education in many states. Thus, the public sector's productivity appears to be a crucial, yet largely unfocused, issue for states.

Third, the neoliberal claims about higher education finance are partially supported by the analysis of state experience. The neoliberal claim that institutions increased tuition to substitute for the loss of federal student aid revenues does not apply to public institutions—which should not be a surprise, given that this claim is usually made by independent colleges (see, e.g., Council for Advancement 1987; National Institute 1987). The other two claims advanced by those who defend the public investment in higher education appear to be supported by available evidence, however. Clearly increases in tuition in public institutions have been fueled by reductions in state support, consistent with neoliberal claims, even though public four-year institutions did gain revenue from federal student aid programs in the process.

Additionally, the analyses of tax revenue returns on public support of higher education provide an interesting new aspect

The public sector's productivity appears to be a crucial, yet largely unfocused, issue for states.

of the political debate about higher education finance, especially in states with progressive income tax systems. Recent studies indicate a positive tax revenue return to states, ranging from about 2:1 in states with progressive state tax systems (Bluestone 1993; Girling, Goldman, and Keith 1993) to 1.13:1 in Texas, a state with a regressive tax system (Creech, Carpenter, and Davis 1994).

Finally, the neo-Marxist claims about the consequences of public financing decisions are supported by the review of available evidence. The research on the effects of prices and price subsidies on enrollment of low-income and minority students is particularly troubling. The financial restructuring of the past 15 years apparently has reduced postsecondary opportunities for low-income and minority students. Further, state officials seem to have nearly totally overlooked this effect (Mingle 1987; State Higher Education 1988). Greater attention to low-income and minority students' attendance would appear to be a crucial issue for states. And it appears that retrenchment in public institutions—the midyear adjustment to reductions in state support—compounds this problem. Institutions are quick to reduce support for programs that serve middle-class professions, the fields that are most accessible to many first-time college students, while maintaining or even improving programs that serve elite professions and corporate interests.

INSTITUTIONAL FINANCING STRATEGIES

Colleges and universities are at the center of the storm of controversy over college costs. The primary focus has been the
reasons why the prices they charge their students have risen
faster than inflation. Neoconservatives have speculated that
college costs have risen because of greed and a general lack
of productivity, while defenders of the academy have pointed
to other issues. In their defense, colleges and universities have
attempted to shift the blame to the states and the federal
government. Beneath the surface of this controversy lingers
a complex set of financial and academic issues. This section
reexamines recent studies on college prices and productivity,
emphasizing the untangling of evidence related to the seemingly contradictory claims about the causes of price increases.

The Institutional Perspective

The controversy over college costs has been especially problematic for colleges and universities. In the 1980s, strategic
planning and management methodologies were widely
adopted in an effort to avoid the financial crisis that had been
predicted (Chaffee 1985, 1989; Hearn 1987). These strategies
apparently helped many small private colleges to avoid clo-
sure and develop new, more distinctive missions (Chaffee
1985; St. John 1991c). During this period, higher education
was confronted with a decline in federal and state support,
in reaction to which colleges and universities raised tuition
and made investments aimed at improving their competitive
positions. It follows that the widespread criticisms of colleges
for raising their prices could be seen as an unanticipated consequence of these developments.

The criticisms caught the higher education community
unprepared. On the one hand:

> *Critics may be tempted to treat tuition rates as yardsticks
> for measuring whether an institution is fiscally responsible
> and responsive to consumer need. They could cite rising
> tuition as proof of institutional inefficiency, irresponsibility,
> or greed* (Council for Advancement 1987, p. 1).

But on the other, increased efficiency would be hard to
realize:

> *Significant campus cost savings can be relatively hard to
> achieve or to communicate, particularly when they occur*

*on the academic side. To publicize freezing or trimming
of departmental budgets, for example, can prove hazardous
because of faculty sensitivities and also because the public
may perceive such cuts as a reduction in quality or scope
of academic programs* (Council for Advancement 1987, p. 2).

This document concentrated on the mechanisms and strategies institutions should use to communicate about rising tuition: whom to contact, what to emphasize in communications
with the press, and so forth. Other documents developed by
associations during this period also focused on how institutions should tell the story about price increases (e.g., Association of Governing Boards 1986; National Institute 1987).

Understanding Price Changes

Two competing explanations are advanced for the incremental
growth in real prices charged by colleges and universities during the past decade: growth in expenditures (and related declines in productivity), and changes in government support.

Growth in expenditures and price increases

Trends in expenditures between 1975 and 1985 have been
analyzed extensively (Kirshstein, Tikoff, et al. 1990; O'Keefe
1987; St. John 1992a). When the analyses control for oscillations in enrollment, they reveal that, in the early 1980s,
educational expenditures rose faster than inflation, both administrative and instructional expenditures increased, and
administrative expenditures increased faster than instructional expenditures.

Trends in tuition and expenditures. From available evidence, it appears these trends have continued though the late
1980s into the early 1990s. Table 5 presents indices for
changes in tuition and expenditures for the period between
academic years 1977 and 1991. Tuition charges (indexed by
the consumer price index) increased substantially faster than
inflation in both public and private institutions between academic years 1981 and 1991. In the late 1970s, tuition actually
declined in public institutions and remained even with inflation in private institutions. So do expenditures explain these
trends?

On the surface, some relationship appears to exist between
expenditures and tuition. Total expenditures per full-time

TABLE 5

INDICES OF SELECTED EXPENDITURES PER FTE STUDENT AND AVERAGE UNDERGRADUATE TUITION CHARGES AT PUBLIC AND PRIVATE UNIVERSITIES (Constant Dollars): Academic Years Ending 1977 through 1991

Academic Year Ending	Tuition Charges	Expenditures		
		Total	Instruction	Admin- istration
PUBLIC UNIVERSITIES				
1977	105	98	99	99
1978	105	99	101	101
1979	103	103	104	104
1980	102	102	102	99
1981	100	100	100	100
1982	104	99	99	100
1983	109	98	99	100
1984	114	101	101	103
1985	116	106	105	113
1986	123	110	108	119
1987	128	112	111	122
1988	128	115	111	124
1989	130	117	111	126
1990	135	117	111	125
1991	136	120	113	127
PRIVATE UNIVERSITIES				
1977	100	97	97	92
1978	99	96	96	92
1979	99	97	97	98
1980	99	99	98	101
1981	100	100	100	100
1982	104	100	102	99
1983	112	101	104	107
1984	118	108	109	118
1985	123	113	112	121
1986	127	117	116	126
1987	134	128	129	139
1988	140	129	127	141
1989	142	131	131	143
1990	147	133	132	141
1991	153	137	138	145

Note: The consumer price index was used to convert tuition charges to constant dollars, the higher education price index to convert expenditures to constant dollars. The analysis used the IPEDS/HEGIS (Integrated Postsecondary Educational Data System/Higher Education General Information Survey)

Source: Alsalam et al. 1993, p. 144.

Prices, Productivity, and Investment

equivalent (FTE) student (indexed by the higher education price index) increased at a faster rate than inflation throughout the 1980s in both public and private institutions. In the public sector, expenditures on instruction increased incrementally during the early 1980s, then remained constant in the late 1980s, while expenditures on administration climbed throughout the decade. In private institutions, expenditures on both instruction and administration increased throughout the ten-year period. It should be noted, however, that neither type of expenditure increased as fast as tuition during the ten years and that administrative expenditures increased faster than instructional expenditures.

Thus, the trends of the early 1980s, which were widely investigated, not only continued during the next half decade, but also seem to have accelerated. Therefore, the analyses of the causes and consequences of increases in expenditures in the early 1980s could be quite relevant to the more recent period. The next subsection attempts to untangle whether these increases in expenditures were a cause or consequence of the increases in tuition.

The link between prices and expenditures. Considerable attention has been given to the link between educational expenditures and tuition charges. The Department of Education's studies of college costs consistently focused on this link, assuming a causal relationship. The first of these studies focused on administrative costs (Snyder and Galambos 1988), echoing earlier criticism of expenditures on administration (Bassett 1983). The report documents the rise in administrative expenditures as a portion of college budgets: "Administrative costs now represent 19.2 percent of education and general expenditure, as compared to 12.5 percent in academic year 1949–50" (Snyder and Galambos 1988, p. 67). Based on case studies of the University of Florida and the University of Georgia, growth in nonteaching professionals was an apparent cause for the increase in administrative expenditures. The study considers a range of explanations for the growth in administrative expenditures, including expansion of professional functions, such as financial aid, and the impact of regulations, but reaches no firm conclusions about the causes of this growth. Additionally, the study makes no attempt to examine the link between expenditures and price increases.

Another study funded by the U.S. Department of Education further explores the causes of growth in educational expenditures and the link between educational expenditures and tuition (Kirshstein, Tikoff, et al. 1990). The analysis of trends in costs considered growth in expenditures on instruction, administration, and plant operations and found that administrative expenditures were influenced by the professionalization of administrative services, growth in faculty salaries and benefits contributed to the expansion in expenditures on instruction, and expenditures for plant operations apparently had not kept pace with needs. Another report examining the link between expenditures and tuition using a regression model reaches the following conclusion:

The results of this model suggest that in the early 1980s, tuition increased not only in response to rising expenditures but also as a means to finance higher education expenditures. According to the same econometric model, in the late 1970s tuition rose in response to budgetary pressures but not as a means to finance additional expenditures (Kirshstein, Sherman, et al. 1990, p. iii).

More generally, the conclusion that the increases in costs have been the primary driver of tuition (Massy and Wilger 1992) has been widely accepted, and states have begun to focus on ways of reducing educational costs (Knutsen 1993). These developments seem to have fueled the financial restructuring of state systems of higher education. In fact, a study of three state systems that underwent retrenchment in 1992–93 found that concerns of state officials about administrative costs were a major force in the state budgeting process (St. John 1993a).

The differences between public and private colleges and universities should not be overlooked. This federally funded research does not distinguish between public and private colleges, and "given the relatively short time period covered by the data, it generally was not possible to measure precisely the relationships between tuition and expenditures across sectors" (Kirshstein, Sherman, et al. 1990, p. 83). The analysis of case studies seems to indicate that when states reduce their institutional support, public institutions reduce their expenditures, focusing first on administrative expenditures (St. John

1992a). This finding supports a different conclusion from the one reached by the federal study:

In this analysis, . . . whether public institutions raised their prices slower or faster than similar institutions was independent of expenditure trends. In contrast, there was a simultaneous occurrence of both of these conditions—rising expenditures and rising prices—in four of the private colleges visited. Thus, these findings do not support the argument that excessive spending is the primary cause of tuition increases . . . and, therefore, such an argument should be treated with caution in the . . . policy debates about higher education finance (St. John 1992a, p. 179).

Specifically, this finding raises an important point for public officials to consider. It raises doubts about the claim that expenditures cause increases in tuition. It is entirely possible that when states severely cut state funding, prices can increase while expenditures decrease, a development that has been recently observed in case studies of state financing practices (Griswold and Marine *In press;* St. John 1992a, 1993a). This prospect raises serious doubts about the wisdom of using cost management strategies as the primary means of public efforts aimed at controlling costs in higher education, because such a strategy can result in an increased price for reduced services, a situation already evident in many public institutions.

A recent econometric study digs beneath the surface to examine the factors that influence changes in expenditures per student. The study not only confirms that administrative expenditures increased faster than academic expenditures, but also explains more completely why expenditures per student increased. First, the competitive nature of the higher education market influenced prices to rise. Institutions that had increased enrollments had lower expenditures per student, while institutions that had declines in enrollment had increased expenditures per student. Further, more than a third of the higher education institutions in the United States had declining enrollments, although demand did not decline overall. Indeed, quite the opposite was the case:

The most striking finding . . . is that one-third of the institutions suffered declines in enrollment even as overall enrollment grew. That so many institutions could lose enroll-

*ment gives a strong indication that market forces bear heav-
ily on institutions of higher education. When institutions
fall out of favor with customers, or when demographics shift
students elsewhere, institutions face loss in revenues. . . .
The marketplace then imposes its discipline. Institutions that
do not deliver services that a sufficient number of students
find attractive must change course or suffer decline* (Getz
and Siegfried 1991, p. 390).

Second, as the overall "demand for higher education increases, the derived demand for the most important input,
faculty, also increase[s], causing a rise in average faculty salaries" (Getz and Siegfried 1991, p. 391). Between 1978–79 and
1987–88, faculty salaries increased by an estimated average
of 1.6 percent per year above the rate of increased prices.
Because student/faculty ratios increased slightly, however,
the gains in faculty salaries were not a major force driving up
costs or prices. The cost of faculty salaries was mitigated to
an extent by increasing class sizes and more part-time faculty
(Getz and Siegfried 1991).

Third, consumer preferences for services like institutional
support, student services, and academic services influenced
institutions to incur extra costs, and other services, such as
fund-raising, also increased. As a result, institutions, especially
private colleges, were "supplying a demonstrably higher-
quality service at a higher cost" (Getz and Siegfried 1991,
p. 391).

Thus, the literature that assumes a link between expenditures and tuition is suspect—especially if the intent is to use
the findings as a basis for public policy. A correlation appears
to exist between educational expenditures and tuition, but
not the direct causal link that the literature claims (e.g., Kirshstein, Sherman, et al. 1990). Some institutions apparently
raised tuition to generate revenue for increasing expenditures,
but in other cases, particularly in the public sector, schools
increased tuition when expenditures declined. Further, expenditures per student have been more likely to rise in institutions that experienced declining enrollments, which was
about a third of the total number of institutions (Getz and
Siegfried 1991). And while some students were willing to pay
more for an improved quality of educational services (Evangelauf 1988a, 1988b; Getz and Siegfried 1991; Kirshstein, Sherman, et al. 1990), the fact remains that poor students were

not able to pay more for reduced quality in low-cost institutions (Freedberg 1993; St. John 1993a). More important, many of the basic assumptions made by neoconservatives about unproductive behavior in academe (e.g., Finn 1988a, 1988b) appear far too simplistic (Getz and Siegfried 1991; St. John 1992a), which raises questions about whether the evidence of simultaneous increases of expenditures and tuition has any practical value for policy makers.

Government support and college prices

Federal student aid policy can indirectly influence changes in prices. Indeed, recent evidence suggests that public institutions can gain revenues from federal student aid programs when they raise tuition (Hearn and Anderson 1989; McPherson and Schapiro 1991). The situation is substantially different in private institutions, however, where the cost provisions in federal programs can limit the amount of additional revenue that can be gained from increased tuition. In fact, in private colleges the reverse situation has been the case: Private institutions increased their own allocations to student aid to compensate for the loss of federal student aid (Council for Advancement 1987; Green 1987; National Institute 1987).

The initial research on the impact of federal student financial assistance on tuition was conducted for the National Commission on Student Financial Assistance (Dickmeyer 1983). Based on a regression analysis, the study concluded that a weak relationship existed between federal student aid and tuition charges in both public and private colleges but cautioned against making generalizations about these relationships. For example, the author observed, the association between tuition and federal funding could be "the result of a statistical artifact and not conscious behavior on the part of college administrators" (Dickmeyer 1983, p. 6).

While these statements indicate that caution should be used in interpreting the findings, the author does not explicitly consider how the eligibility requirements for federal student aid programs might limit the revenue gains associated with tuition increases. In other words, just because the amount of revenue from federal student aid is correlated with tuition charges, it does not mean that institutions can gain revenue from increasing their tuition charges. Nevertheless, the findings of this study—not the cautionary notes—seem to have influenced neoconservatives.

Two more recent econometric studies examine the relationship between government student aid and tuition charges. One study of the relationship between pricing decisions and student aid concludes that:

> . . . (1) with regard to federal student aid, we find that, at private four-year institutions, increases in SEOG [Supplemental Educational Opportunity Grant] and Pell expenditures do not cause schools to raise tuition and fees, although increases in federal financial aid do lead to higher tuition and fees in public four-year institutions; (2) federal grants and contracts have important effects on tuition and fees, institution-based financial aid, and instructional expenditures throughout higher education—our results indicate that cutbacks in research funding would lead to higher tuition at private four-year institutions, lower institutional financial aid at four-year private, and both four-year and two-year public institutions, and lower instructional expenditures for all three groups; and (3) increases in state and local appropriations significantly increase instructional spending in three of the institutional categories examined (McPherson and Schapiro 1991, p. 74).

Another econometric study also suggests the reverse of Secretary Bennett's claim, concluding that ". . . increases in federal grants to students would decrease the rate of growth in tuition" (Paulsen 1991, p. 355). Further, regarding the influence of state financial support, ". . . increases in state and local government appropriations to public institutions would decrease the rate of growth in tuition" (p. 355).

The effects of price changes

Recent analyses of students' responses to prices strongly indicate that prices and price subsidies influence students' enrollment behavior (St. John 1990a, 1990b: St. John and Starkey *In press*). In an effort to assess the effect of actual price changes in the early 1980s (FY1981 to FY1986), actual changes in tuition and institutional allocations to grants and price-response measures derived for the study of student enrollment behavior in the early 1980s were used to estimate the effects of changes in institutional pricing policy (St. John 1993b). The study found that changes in institutional aid in private colleges apparently helped mitigate the effects of price increases, as did federal loan dollars. In public four-year institutions, however, the changes in both grants and tuition would have decreased enrollment if federal loans had not partially mitigated this force. And in public two-year institutions, federal grants actually helped increase enrollments (St. John 1993b). Apparently, available maximum Pell awards went farther toward paying tuition at public two-year colleges. (The reader is cautioned that these analyses were an approximation of the effects of changes in prices and subsidies based on the results of price-response studies [St. John 1990a, 1990b] rather than a trend analysis of these effects [e.g., McPherson and Schapiro 1991].) The two types of studies did, however, reach similar conclusions.

Understanding Productivity

In criticizing colleges for raising their tuition, some observers have raised questions about the productivity of administrators and faculty (Finn 1988a, 1988b; Iosue 1988; Snyder and Galambos 1988). The basic production ratios in higher education—student/faculty ratios and so on—have increased slightly over time, but productivity is exceedingly difficult to measure and to regulate in higher education.

Problems with measuring productivity

Research on productivity and efficiency in higher education has been plagued by problems with the measurement of inputs and, especially, outputs. Indeed, the word "productivity" seems to have taken a symbolic meaning in many states that has a negative influence on the state's budget process (Layzell and Lyddon 1990).

> *The major problem is that of defining and measuring the outputs of the colleges and universities. Unfortunately, the literature provides very little help in solving the problem. The result is that any empirical study of higher education production and cost behavior will be limited by the crudeness of the output measures used and the study will be open to criticism on that basis* (Carlson 1977, p. 7).

This problem with measurement has continued to plague research on efficiency and productivity in higher education. Most research has focused on expenditures per student, but expenditures per student provide very little indication of

In contrast, the literature on teaching productivity is more sparse. Faculty's instructional innovations apparently are influenced by individual motivation, not monetary rewards (Davis et al. 1982). Further, only a slight link is apparent between research productivity and teaching. A meta-analysis of studies that examined the effects of research productivity on teaching concludes that research had a consistent and slight positive effect on teaching effectiveness (Feldman 1987).

Recent studies have argued that the quality of instruction has declined, which has been attributable to increases in "discretionary time," a phenomenon fueled by an "academic rachet" of egalitarian appeals for equal treatment (Massy and Zemsky 1992). A critical analysis of this phenomenon argues that market forces have influenced the trend toward more discretionary time and that institutions need to emphasize undergraduate teaching more (Winston 1994).

Thus, the research on faculty productivity provides some insights into the reasons for the lingering problem of academic productivity: Faculty are rewarded more for their research than for their teaching. The internal structure of incentives of the academy simply does not value instructional innovation and productivity in the same way it values research productivity and reputation. These conditions inhibit even marginal reductions in instructional costs. Further, market forces in the academic community fuel this problem. Clearly, an understanding of this internal structure of incentives—and its influence on the value system of faculty—should be integral to the envisioning of alternative strategies for reduction of instructional costs.

An alternative approach

Despite these recurrent limitations and impediments, the prospect of using information on productivity as a basis of public (and institutional) policy choices in higher education could have merit. Despite problems with the measurement of productivity, productive behaviors can be identified. The problem is that faculty and administrators have few incentives to engage in behaviors that could actually reduce unit costs. This condition does not exist, at least to the same extent, in private enterprise.

Although the evidence on institutional efficiency is relatively limited, we believe it is possible to identify institutions [that]

use their resources in a relatively efficient manner to pro-
duce observable and measurable outcomes. We believe it
is possible to describe these relatively efficient institutions
by conventional economic production functions [that]
represent the efficient production possibilities, even though
most academic institutions share a value system of relative
inefficiency—that is, administrators and faculty generally
seek higher faculty salaries, lower faculty workloads, smaller
classes, and lower student/faculty ratios. From the student
or government point of view, these pressures against rel-
atively efficient resource use should raise serious questions
about the likely impact of the financial support they provide
these institutions as clients (Weathersby et al. 1977, p. 531).

An expansion on this logic argues that institutions should seek
to align their choices with student goals and reduce their costs
(Weathersby and Jacobs 1977).

This line of argument recognizes that the goals of administrators and faculty are not necessarily aligned with those of
students and taxpayers. The authors assumed, however, that
market forces will influence change, a situation that has not
evolved in the way the authors envisioned, despite a decade
of criticism. A new form of competition did emerge, however:
Proprietary schools have expanded dramatically because of
their vocational offerings. And instead of responding to
general public concerns about costs, many private colleges
developed new marketing strategies targeted at middle-
income students. They adjusted to students' goals by expanding services and student aid. Most public colleges, however,
did not substantially change their marketing and pricing strategies. As a consequence of these developments, access was
diminished for many low-income students.

Government, student, and public concerns about costs are
now emerging (Layzell and Lyddon 1990). Whether these concerns are serious and will be sustained have yet to be determined, but available evidence suggests that public officials
are serious (Jacobson 1992). The basic problems with the
structure of incentives in the academy, which supports behaviors that raise costs per student rather than reduce them, must
be confronted if these basic inefficiencies are to be contended with.

A recently proposed approach could help policy makers,
faculty, and administrators contend with this dilemma—fo-

cusing more explicitly on using inquiry to promote gains in productivity:

> *What is clear is that information on cost savings and improvements in productivity must be based upon systematic analysis of activities at the institutional or departmental level, including different approaches to accountability and incentives. The literature on the subject is . . . meager and provides only some general directions that might be pursued. Moreover, no generic approach is likely to provide identical results across different institutional settings, subjects, and applications. This suggests a need for colleges and universities and their constituent departments to experiment with various accountability and incentive strategies and instructional strategies, including not only instructional technologies, but also various configurations of large-group and small-group instruction, peer tutoring, cooperative learning, and other techniques* (Levin 1991, p. 258).

An experimental approach to improving productivity, one that places greater emphasis on understanding the incentives for faculty and administrators, certainly has merit, although few practical examples of such practices exist. Such an approach would seem especially "productive" if it were coupled with a strategy that emphasizes students' learning and development of the whole student.

Higher Education as an Investment
The public's concerns about productivity in higher education are linked to their concerns about the amount of tax dollars used to support higher education and the costs of attending. Therefore, the issue of return on investment is important to colleges and universities on two levels: the return for taxpayers and the return for individual consumers. Colleges and universities should consider these issues more explicitly when they develop arguments for more government support for operations and student aid, as well as when they assess the effects of their efforts to market their services to students.

From the perspective of the average consumer, higher education remains a good investment. And this benefit can be communicated.

> *The popular image of the unemployed honors graduate who returns home with a bag full of laundry and an unpaid*

loan to reclaim his old room dissipates as . . . a chart and . . . data—not anecdotes—[are used] to tell the story about the relationship between education and income (Williams 1993).

Colleges and universities cannot afford, however, to price their services based on the individual's expected return, as students respond to prices based on the actual prices they pay. The percentage of the population that can afford the full costs of the average private college is severely limited. And while the percentage of the population that can afford the average public tuition is substantially larger, the average student attending a public four-year college or public two-year college is highly price-sensitive (St. John, Oescher, and Andrieu 1992; St. John and Starkey 1994). Unless price increases in either sector are accompanied by increases in need-based financial aid, then the percentage of the potential population that can afford to attend college will shrink. Thus, within the constraints of the current financing arrangements for public and private higher education, the fact that higher education has high individual returns has limited value to institutions. The market itself constrains the extent to which most institutions can raise prices (Garvin 1980; Getz and Siegfried 1991). Even sustained movement toward a high-tuition, high-aid strategy would eventually cease to draw students when the sticker price gets too high.

The prospect that institutions can sell the government on increasing its investments in institutional and student subsidies is doubtful, however, unless their arguments are tied to taxpayers' concerns about improving the rate of return on the public investment. While emerging research consistently indicates that tax revenue returns are positive (Bluestone 1993; Creech, Carpenter, and Davis 1994; Girling, Goldman, and Keith 1993), this fact alone might not be a sufficient basis for institutions and their representatives to argue for increases in state subsidies and state and federal allocations to student aid.

Assessing Ideological Claims

The conventional conservative and liberal claims about the public investment in higher education are not germane to the oscillations in college and university tuition during the past 14 years. Rather, they are useful in interpreting the meaning of the underlying financial restructuring. In the early 1980s, the percentage of the total economic cost of higher education that was borne by government declined from 49 percent in 1975 to 43 percent in 1980, 36 percent in 1985, and 34 percent in 1990. At the same time, the percentage of the burden borne by families rose from 39 percent in 1975 to 43 percent in 1980 and 49 percent in 1985 and 1990 (National Commission on Responsibilities 1993, p. 23). The shift in the burden for financing higher education—from the government to students and their families—was consonant with conventional conservative arguments about the economic value of higher education, which accrue primarily to the individual, and the belief that these costs should be borne primarily by individuals. Further, the shift in emphasis between grants and loans was also consonant with this argument. Whether this claim is correct or not remains subject to debate and interpretation.

First, two of the claims made by neoconservatives pertain directly to changes in higher education finance during the 1980s. Both of the neoconservative claims about higher education institutions had some factual basis, but the Reagan and Bush administrations' interpretations misrepresented the facts. The first of these claims was that institutions raised tuition to gain more federal student financial aid. Private colleges, the sector of higher education with the highest tuition and the most substantial increases, did not gain federal grant revenue when they raised tuition. The cost provisions of federal grant programs would preclude it. Further, the fact that federal grants were declining meant not only that there were no more grant revenues to gain, but also that institutions were adjusting to revenue losses. Because their prices were lower, public colleges could theoretically gain more grant revenue than they might otherwise if they raised tuition. Public institutions generally raised tuition to compensate for losses in state appropriations, however, rather than to gain Pell revenue. Because of the cuts in federal grant programs, public four-year colleges actually lost scholarship grant revenue from external sources in the early 1980s (St. John 1993b). And when tuition increased incrementally in public four-year colleges, enrollments of low-income students declined. Thus, the neoconservative claim that institutions raised tuition to increase revenue from federal grants seems ill conceived and apparently based on incomplete information.

The claim that institutions raised tuition to increase revenue from federal grants seems ill conceived and based on incomplete information.

The neoconservative claim that colleges and universities raised tuition because they were unproductive and wasteful is also a misrepresentation of the facts. While colleges and universities are not productive organizations, their productivity ratios changed very little in the 1980s. Instructional and administrative expenditures increased incrementally in the 1980s. The growth in instructional expenditures was attributable primarily to growth in faculty salaries and benefits, while the growth in administrative expenditures appears to be related to incremental growth in professional nonteaching positions. The growth in the professionalization of college administrators, however, apparently helped many private colleges avert financial crises (St. John 1991c, 1992a). Nevertheless, the criticisms raised by the neoconservatives raised public awareness of the longstanding unproductive economic behavior of colleges and universities.

The average production costs in higher education are higher than is necessary to educate postsecondary students. They are high because of historic production functions—the ratios of students to faculty, class sizes, and so forth—that have been maintained despite the increased availability of new instructional technologies (such as telecommunications, computers, and television). Thus, a challenge faces colleges and universities, one with long historical roots, to reduce production costs to better meet taxpayers' and students' needs. Further, the neoconservative criticisms about productivity are only the tip of the iceberg. Higher education faces some very basic problems regarding production costs and the related prices. The remedies to the problems of productivity facing the academy will necessarily involve faculty as part of the solution, however (Levin 1991), rather than the type of central actions advocated by the neoconservatives (U.S. Dept. of Education ca. 1990).

Second, two of the neoliberal claims about higher education finance that emerged in response to neoconservative criticisms of higher education in the 1980s are germane to the issues of pricing and productivity. The neoliberal claim, that institutions raised tuition to compensate for the loss of federal grant dollars, was made primarily by private colleges and universities. This claim is supported by the evidence reviewed here, at least for private colleges. Private colleges did raise their internal grant allocations as a means of compensating for losses in federal grants, which helped them mitigate the potential negative effects of changes in federal student aid policy. This claim does not hold for public colleges and universities, however, where grants were not increased to adjust to the new conditions. Additionally, the neoliberal claim that public institutions raised tuition to compensate for losses of state appropriations is supported by available evidence. These developments, however, had a negative influence on enrollment of low-income and minority students, as increases in federal grants did not keep pace with increases in tuition in public institutions.

Thus, the two forces identified by institutions as part of their neoliberal defense—that shifts in state and federal financial strategies influenced increases in tuition—seem to have had as much or more influence on the incremental increases in prices than the incremental erosions of institutional productivity identified by the neoconservatives. Further, the fact that market forces influenced changes in expenditures (Getz and Siegfried 1991) further reduces the legitimacy of the claim that losses in productivity caused increases in tuition.

UNDERSTANDING FINANCIAL STRATEGY

Before assessing alternative financial strategies, it is important to think critically about the conceptual models used to routinely assess financial alternatives. As the preceding sections illustrate, the conceptual bases chosen by analysts and policy makers to make arguments for policy alternatives are influenced by their political beliefs. Therefore, it is necessary to examine critically the validity of the embedded theoretical claims in the models typically used in analyses of financial strategy in higher education to construct a more workable conceptual framework for assessing future choices about financial strategy. This section undertakes an intermediate reconstruction of the models typically used to assess financial strategies in higher education, first critically examining four theories that are frequently used in analyses of financial strategy in higher education—human capital theory, revenue theory, political incrementalism, and critical theory. Then the conclusions reached from this analysis are used to propose a reconstructed model for assessing financial strategy.

The Limits of Extant Theories

The findings from the review can be used to examine critically the theoretical claims embedded in the literature on higher education finance, a necessary step in the development of a reconstructed understanding of how we might improve the strategies commonly used to assess financial strategies.

Human capital theory

It is important to examine critically the assumptions embedded in human capital theory, precisely because human capital theory is consistently used as a basis for policy proposals. A study of testimony before Congress for reauthorizations of the Higher Education Act found that college and university presidents frequently used arguments based on human capital in their congressional testimony (Slaughter 1991). And a recent study of state influence on higher education financial restructuring found that arguments based on human capital had a great influence on the development of state plans (St. John 1993a), a development that is entirely consistent with theory on higher education master planning (Halstead 1974). Further, recent research on state and federal responsibilities in the financing of higher education holds certain assumptions based on human capital (e.g., Kramer 1993a). Clearly, human capital theory has a substantial influence on the formulation of policy proposals for the financing of higher education.

Theoretical claims. Human capital theory (Becker 1964) views decisions to invest in education as a choice with costs and benefits, both pecuniary and nonpecuniary. For individuals, the pecuniary costs include the direct costs of attending (tuition, books, living expenses, and so on) and opportunity costs (i.e., foregone earnings), while the primary pecuniary benefits include gains in lifetime earnings. Nonpecuniary benefits include satisfaction with work and related social and psychological benefits. For society, the pecuniary costs include both the direct expenditures of tax dollars—the subsidies provided to institutions and, more recently, to students—and indirect, or opportunity, costs associated with the decreased opportunity to make other investments (for example, in defense, police and fire protection, and so forth), while the benefits include gains in productivity and tax revenues. The nonpecuniary benefits to society include intergenerational equity and an increased sense of democracy. Additionally, subsidized loan programs could reduce an individual's direct costs and thus increase opportunities to attend college (Becker 1964).

This basic paradigm has been variously interpreted in the academic and political debates over higher education finance. Research examining the public and private costs and benefits of direct public subsidies of higher education institutions (Leslie and Brinkman 1988) was particularly influential in the public choices to emphasize federal programs that subsidized students rather than programs that subsidized institutions (Gladieux and Wolanin 1976; National Commission on the Financing 1973). The conventional liberal interpretation of human capital theory has emphasized gains in productivity as the pecuniary benefit and intergenerational equity as the social benefit (Kramer 1993a). A recent neoliberal claim is that tax revenues provide a possible basis for justifying federal spending (e.g., Bluestone 1993; Creech, Carpenter, and Davis 1994; Girling, Goldman, and Keith 1993; St. John and Masten 1990). If this measure is used in estimates of costs and benefits, then the broader measure of productivity of the workforce cannot be used without double counting benefits.

Thus, a set of claims is embedded in human capital theory, as it has evolved.

- The individual's return on investment includes gains in lifetime earnings (a claim that is certainly supported by the research literature).
- Society's return from the public investment is gains in the state or national product (a claim that has historically been difficult to measure and interpret).
- Society's return includes gains in tax revenues derived from individual gains in lifetime earnings, a claim that is considered double counting if one also considers gains in productivity (recent research suggests this approach has merit, although further refinements in methods used in this kind of analysis are certainly possible).
- Student aid functions as a means of reducing individual costs for needy students (while this assumption holds when critically examined at a general level, the net price concept, which has been frequently used to estimate the effects of prices, is problematic).

The theoretical assumptions embedded in human capital theory have generally held up when examined in empirical studies, which is one reason it has been frequently used in planning and budgeting. Human capital theory has some limitations, however, that merit consideration when reconstructing the theory of higher education finance.

Limitations. The strict application of human capital theory has at least three major limitations that are evident from a review of the controversy over higher education costs. First, human capital theory does not explicitly address the issue of organizational productivity in higher education. An analyst using human capital theory might assume that market forces would influence institutions to assume competitive behaviors. But the history of higher education of the past several decades indicates that the incentives in the academy, which are based on widely held assumptions about academic excellence, do not promote productivity. A college or university, or even an academic program, that exhibited highly efficient and productive behavior, such as having high student/faculty ratios and high rates of student achievement and degree completion, would probably run into problems with accrediting agencies because of those ratios.

Second, the development of price-response theory, especially the concept of net price, does not adequately explain the enrollment behavior of students. Standardized student price-response coefficients (SPRCs) (Jackson and Weathersby 1975; Leslie and Brinkman 1988; McPherson 1978; National Commission on the Financing 1973) have evolved as a means of linking enrollments and changes in prices (and subsidies). These methods have not adequately predicted enrollments, however. A review of the literature argues that other forces explain why SPRCs did not adequately explain enrollment behavior (Leslie and Brinkman 1988). Recent research indicates that students respond to several types of prices and that the way they respond to prices can be influenced by changes in financing policy (St. John 1993b; St. John and Starkey *In press*). Therefore, the topic of student price response merits critical thought and analysis.

Third, human capital theory does not adequately depict important constraints on equity in the social system. Specifically, human capital theory seems to hold that economic constraints are the primary inhibitor of opportunity, but minority students appear to have less than an equal opportunity to attend college (St. John 1991d; Tierney 1992) because of a variety of barriers. Further, even when African-Americans attain an education, their earnings are not always on the same level as others with an equal level of education (Pascarella and Terenzini 1991). Thus, models used to assess the effects of financial policies need to account for these other forces.

Revenue theory

Revenue theory, developed as an explanation for economic behavior within academic organizations (Bowen 1980), is germane to the discussion of higher education finance because it has been widely used as a basis for analyses of cost trends in higher education (e.g., Kirshstein, Sherman, et al. 1990; Kirshstein, Tikoff, et al. 1990), as well as for politically motivated criticisms of higher education spending.

Theoretical claims. The revenue theory of higher education costs makes the following claims:

1. *The dominant goals of higher education are educational excellence, prestige, and influence.*
2. *In quest of excellence, prestige, and influence, there is virtually no limit to the amount of money an institution could spend on seemingly fruitful educational ends.*

3. *Each institution raises all the money it can.*
4. *Each institution spends all it raises.*
5. *The cumulative effect of the preceding four laws is toward ever-increasing expenditures* (Bowen 1980, pp. 19, 20).

Neoconservatives used Bowen's theory extensively as a basis for their criticism of the higher education community's raising its prices in the 1980s. Two basic claims are embedded in Bowen's theory: (1) In their quest for excellence, institutions will raise all the revenue they can; and (2) institutions will spend all they raise. According to Bowen, the pursuit of excellence is the motive for these behaviors. Neoconservatives, however, reinterpreted these claims to mean that (3) institutions are greedy and unproductive and (4) they raised tuition to support their spending habits. A big difference exists, however, between claim 1 and interpretation 3 as to institutions' motives and between claim 2 and interpretation 4 as to the connection between revenues and expenditures. To untangle this mess, it is necessary to examine the four claims separately.

First, substantial evidence supports the assumption (claim 1) that institutions will raise all the money they can. Clearly, the incentive structure of administrators and faculty discussed earlier seems to support this claim. But the tendency for public institutions to raise their tuition to substitute for the loss of state revenue indicates that institutions could have raised tuition higher in the past (Garvin 1980), a situation that seems to mitigate this claim. The fact, however, that a scheme was developed to help guide colleges and universities in their efforts to generate alternate revenue sources also supports claim 1 (National Association 1988). Thus, this claim appears generally correct, but it does not necessarily appear to be the basis for pricing decisions.

Second, evidence also supports the assumption (claim 2) that institutions will spend the revenue they generate—in the general pattern of trends in expenditures (Kirshstein, Tikoff, et al. 1990) and in the various attempts to develop case studies (O'Keefe 1987; St. John 1992a). When institutions had sufficient revenues, they increased spending on instruction and administration. But when they did not have sufficient total revenue, they constrained their expenditures, especially their expenditures on administration (O'Keefe 1987; St. John 1992a). Thus, the research supports the conclusion that a link exists between general revenue levels and spending patterns: Spending is influenced by revenues.

Third, the research only partially supports the neoconservative notion (interpretation 3) that institutions raised tuition because they were unproductive and greedy. The facts are that, historically, institutions of higher education have not been highly productive, they have absorbed new technologies without making gains in productivity, and the incentive structure within the academy does not support instructional productivity. The implicit assertion that institutions are unproductive because of greed is not supported by history or recent research. While faculty salaries gained some ground in the early 1980s, they did little more than make up for ground lost in the 1970s (Kirshstein, Tikoff, et al. 1990). Further, faculty members' choice to teach frequently means that they will earn less than they might if they used their education for other purposes, as the incentive structure in the academy supports research productivity rather than instructional productivity. Moreover, changes in productivity in the 1980s were influenced by market forces (Getz and Siegfried 1991); thus, the assertion that greed was a motive seems ill-founded, as though it represents a misinterpretation of revenue theory and the facts. And incremental decreases in productivity were but one factor influencing increases in tuition. The fact remains, however, that neoconservatives raised the issue of productivity and, in so doing, have influenced public attitudes, making productivity a symbolic political issue that institutions must reckon with if they are to avoid escalation of the problems inherent in the financial restructuring now under way in higher education.

Finally, the neoconservative assertion (interpretation 4) that colleges and universities raised tuitions to support their spending habits simply is not supported by available evidence. A correlation undoubtedly exists between expenditures and trends in tuition, but on closer examination it is also evident that increases in tuition were influenced by decreases in the federal government's support of its grant programs, decreases in state subsidies for institutions, and perceptions of demand from students; and that some institutions increased tuition but reduced spending, especially institutions with constraints on other sources of revenue. More generally, the overall pattern of revenue substitution seems to mitigate the link between any single source of revenue and spending. Thus, this neoconservative interpretation of revenue theory seems to have been a deception aimed at diverting public attention from the fact that reductions in federal spending on grant programs had contributed to increases in tuition in the private sector.

Limitations. The limits of revenue theory should be readily evident from this review. First, revenue theory is a reasonably accurate description of institutional behavior, but it is a description that can easily lead to misinterpretations. Further, the theoretical claims embedded in revenue theory seem to be valid when critically examined, while neoconservatives' related interpretations do not hold up when critically examined.

Second, revenue theory does not adequately articulate the incentive structure within the academic community. It depicts the phenomena of raising and spending money, practices at which faculty and administrators have proven to be quite skillful, but it does not adequately explain why they are. Specifically, the interests of faculty and administrators are represented by smaller classes, lower student/faculty ratios, and more staff support. These facts are not evident from the statement of revenue theory, yet these incentives help explain the apparently unproductive behavior of the academy better than the assertion that greed is the motive for spending. A better understanding of these internal mechanisms is needed if productivity is to surface as a viable issue in the academy.

Third, revenue theory ignores the fact that students and potential students respond to prices and price subsidies. The neoconservatives who held and reinterpreted the assumptions of revenue theory also assumed that prices had no influence on students' enrollment decisions, but a logical connection indeed seems to exist between these assumptions. The research on the influence of prices and price subsidies strongly supports the conclusion that students *do* respond to prices. Revenue theory is therefore troubling to the extent that it is used as a basis for policy decisions because of its tacit reinforcement of false assumptions about the relationship between prices and expenditures.

Fourth, revenue theory does not offer a basis for making public policy decisions about higher education finance. When policy makers hold these assumptions, they quickly leap to assertions that more control and regulation are needed. For example, the Clinton administration's attempts to force ac-

Revenue theory does not adequately articulate the incentive structure within the academic community.

crediting agencies to monitor loan defaults (Zook 1994a) and the Reagan and Bush administrations' attempts to regulate defaults appear to be based on the assumption that regulation is the best means of controlling costs.

Political incrementalism

The concept of political incrementalism emanates from the work of Lindblom (1977) and Wildavsky (1979, 1984). Researchers working in this tradition attempt to maintain an objective point of view in their analyses of policy processes but do not assume a rational basis exists for policy decisions. This approach to policy analysis is germane to the cost controversy in higher education, because it generally provides a better explanation of the way policy decisions are made than do rational decision models (Hearn 1993; Layzell and Lyddon 1990). For example, an examination of the reasons for the paradox in the financing of federal Title IV programs using a range of policy models found that, while Title IV funding has grown since its inception, these programs have lacked the philosophical and other bases for such growth (Hearn 1993). The conclusion is that Wildavsky's arguments about rationality with political constraints (1979) seem to explain the paradox:

> *Placed within the context of federal student aid, Wildavsky's idea of dual modes may help inform our understanding of the paradox. It seems reasonable to argue that the paradox stems from an excessive domination of the social interaction mode over the cognition mode* (Hearn 1993, p. 143).

Theoretical claims. Three of the theoretical claims embedded in political incrementalism are germane to this critical analysis of the theoretical bases for reconstructing higher education financial theory: policy changes are made incrementally, policy decisions are influenced by politics instead of (or in addition to) rational analyses, and social interaction and cognition interact in the policy process.

First, this review consistently supports the fundamental theoretical claim of incrementalism, that policy changes are made incrementally in reaction to conditions as they develop, rather than as a result of systematic policy processes (Braybrook and Lindblom 1963; Lindblom 1977). The recent analyses of state budgets and budgeting processes consistently illustrate that state budgeting decisions are based on financial conditions that develop, rather than as a result of "master plans" (Hearn and Griswold 1994; Hines 1988, 1993; Layzell and Lyddon 1990). Indeed, it appears that rational analyses are most appropriately conceived of as subordinate to, and in support of, a budget process that establishes policy. In this context, the incremental annual budget is appropriately viewed as a policy document (Layzell and Lyddon 1990).

Second, the political incrementalist's assumption that policy decisions are made as part of a political process in which rational models and analyses play a subsidiary role (Braybrook and Lindblom 1963; Lindblom 1977; Wildavsky 1979) is partially supported. Historically, these approaches to examining the policy process have indicated that the political process, rather than rational models and analyses, has influenced policy decisions in the federal (Hearn 1993) and state (St. John 1991a) policy arenas, although rational models and analyses have been used in the political process in some interesting instances—for example, the National Commission on the Financing of Postsecondary Education's analyses (1973), which influenced congressional decisions not to fund the federal institutional subsidy program under Title I of the Higher Education Act (federal subsidies to institutions), as amended in 1972 (Gladieux and Wolanin 1976). Additionally, a partial reconstruction of net price theory (Hearn and Longanecker 1985) apparently influenced the emergence of Minnesota's new financing strategy in the middle 1980s (Hearn and Anderson 1989; St. John 1991a; St. John and Elliott 1994). Thus, while federal and state policy processes are essentially political, as the political incremental model claims, rational models and analyses can play a useful role in this process, as instrumental tools in the political discourse.

Third, available evidence also supports the theoretical claim that dual modes of the policy process—social interaction and cognition—interact in the policy process. The social interaction mode has dominated over the cognition mode in the federal student aid policy arena (Hearn 1993), and this review provides further insights into these dual modes of policy deliberation and choice. In the 1980s, social interaction in the higher education policy arena at the federal and state levels changed dramatically with the emergence of neoconservative policy makers and policy analysts. Their criticisms again raised questions about the productivity of colleges and universities that merit consideration. Further, while their analyses seem to be ideologically motivated, they used new theoretical models to develop and interpret their analytic studies. Thus, this review illustrates that the cognition mode became a tool of ideological interests in the politics of the policy process.

Limitations. The political incremental models hold great value for those who aim to understand the process of policy making in higher education (or other arenas). These models, as they are usually formulated, however, have two major limitations.

First, because incremental models generally attempt to maintain objectivity, they often do not fully deal with the influence of ideology. This study has attempted to make this link more explicit than is usually the case in policy studies on higher education finance. In doing so, it has become evident that ideology provides a tacit set of assumptions through which policy analysts and policy makers mediate between the social interaction mode and the cognition mode. The cognition mode—the rational analyses of policy choices (the theoretical basis for analyses and policy proposals)—is influenced by ideological assumptions that are not open to public testing. Thus, policy analysts put together analytic studies that support the political positions of the policy makers for whom they work—studies that rationalize ideological positions, rather than openly examining their own ideological assumptions. It appears, then, that as long as policy making is governed by strategic thinking—goal-directed planning and analysis (Habermas 1984; St. John and Elliott 1994)—the social interaction mode will continue to dominate the cognition mode and rational analysis will remain an instrument of ideologues.

Second, while political incremental models are extremely useful in discerning how various forces influence eventual policy decisions, the need for analytic studies that use reconstructed rational models continues. They are particularly valuable in studies of policy implementation because this perspective can help untangle why policies did not achieve their intended aims. They illuminate the various forces in social and organizational contexts that influence the local implementation of policy decisions. They generally do not, however, provide mechanisms for conducting applied policy studies, and the need for rational models, such as revenue theory or human capital theory therefore continues. To be useful in policy making, however, these models require ongoing adjustment to accommodate the incremental nature of policy making.

Critical theory

Critical theory is diverse and complex. Two recent developments in the application of critical theory in the literature on higher education policy seem germane to this study. First, a neo-Marxist perspective has been used to examine how the political economy and the patriarchal system influence policy choices. This strand of research has added insights into the consequences of financial retrenchment and restructuring in higher education (Gumport 1993; Rhoades 1993; Slaughter 1993a, 1993b). Second, some emergent research focuses on how the assumptions of administrators and faculty influence organizational behavior in higher education (Tierney 1992, 1993). This strand has great potential in untangling how the beliefs of policy makers, administrators, and faculty influence financial decisions in higher education.

Theoretical claims. First, several critical analyses concentrate on the class dialectic, which emanates from emerging neo-Marxist thinking. Essentially, this claim is that upper classes in society oppress the lower classes, and others lacking political power, through political and economic processes. For example, recent studies of retrenchment in higher education (Gumport 1993; Rhoades 1993; Slaughter 1993a, 1993b) demonstrate that elite majors generally receive preferential treatment during retrenchment. This study also treats the issue of the decline in the participation rate of African-Americans and other underrepresented minorities through the lens of the class dialectic. Viewed from this vantage, it appears that minorities were the losers in the restructuring of federal student aid programs that took place in the late 1970s and early 1980s, and that corrections were made through the political influence of affiliated political constituencies, rather than as a result of analytic studies of the consequences of federal policy decisions (see, e.g., Pelavin and Kane 1988). Indeed, the Marxist assumption of a class dialectic generally holds when critically examined in the modern context (Habermas 1987).

The assumption that emerges from the review of research conducted in the second strand of critical studies (i.e., Tierney

1992, 1993) is that social integration is a mechanism through which the discriminatory aspects of the class dialectic take shape. In particular, research into and findings about administrators' assumptions about the social integration of Native Americans (Tierney 1992) and the social attitudes held by students and faculty about gays and lesbians that limit the social and academic freedom of these groups on campus are particularly germane to the reconstruction process in policy making for higher education. Specifically, the current study has found that all of the major constituencies—federal policy makers and their contractors, state higher education executive officers, national higher education associations, administrators and faculty—have held theoretical and ideological assumptions that have gone largely untested in the analysis of higher education policy issues. Thus, the shared beliefs of various constituencies enable them to form communities of inquiry with self-sealing assumptions. These belief systems seem to preclude authentic efforts to achieve new, better-informed understandings.

Limitations. Of course, critical theory has its limitations. First, critical theory that explores issues related to the class dialectic consistently finds inequities, which could mean injustices of some type are embedded in virtually any policy choice. It appears that policy processes involve winners and losers and that those with less political capital generally are the losers. This understanding by itself, however, provides little insight into possible remedies, a limitation that critical theorists openly acknowledge (Slaughter 1993a).

Second, the discovery that social integration is a mechanism through which injustices are replicated is a crucial insight, but by itself it has limited value unless some means is available of transforming the underlying belief systems. After 40 years of efforts to desegregate educational systems in the United States, it appears that political mechanisms have done little to alter the replicating social integration mechanisms that foster inequity (see, e.g., Tierney 1992; Wilson 1986). Thus, it appears that legal and regulatory mechanisms have limited capacity to change these dysfunctional patterns. Further, some analysts entirely ignore social policies that can remedy inequities in their analyses of inequitable situations (e.g., Chaikind ca. 1987; Pelavin and Kane 1988). Therefore, an awareness of the power and dysfunctionalities of the social integration mode of the policy process does not lead to simple solutions, but rather shines a light on the deeper forces that require scrutiny and action.

A Reconstruction of Theory
This critical review of extant theory leads to an intermediate set of understandings that are, in essence, hypotheses about policy making in higher education.

Human capital formation
Understanding 1. *The economic forces embedded in human capital formation provide a basis for the design and assessment of financial strategies in higher education, but this construct needs to be refined to make more explicit links between attainment and the mechanisms that promote productivity and affordability.*

Four conclusions emerging from the critical analysis of human capital theory appear crucial to a reconstruction of the human capital models used to assess financial strategy in higher education.

First, the fact that students and prospective students respond to price subsidies as well as to prices provides a basis for integrating an emphasis on affordability into the methods used to assess financial strategies. Recent research indicates that students respond, not to a single net price, but to a set of prices and price subsidies (Dresch 1975; St. John 1993b; St. John and Starkey *In press*). Further, evidence suggests that minority students are more responsive than whites to prices and price subsidies (Kaltenbaugh 1993, St. John 1991d; St. John and Noell 1989). A differentiated prices approach was recently proposed as an alternative to net price (St. John and Starkey *In press*), based on a review of the research and theoretical arguments developed by Dresch (1975) and Hearn and Longanecker (1985). The alternative approach makes certain basic assumptions:

1. Students might respond differently to price subsidies (grants, loans, and work) than they do to prices (tuition, room, and board).
2. Students' response to prices might change over time as a result of changes in financial strategies, the labor market, and student choice.

3. Students and potential students with different financial means might respond to prices in different ways, depending on the combination of prices and price subsidies they actually face.
4. Frequent research is needed on the effects of prices and price subsidies to determine how changes in financial policies influence the first-time enrollment and persistence decisions of students.
5. The development of price-response measures must be tailored to the context, using appropriate research as a base.
6. The pricing process (setting tuitions and aid policies and estimating the effects of those policies) is a recursive process, with changes in policy influencing the ways students respond to changes in price. Thus, the assessment of pricing alternatives (changes in tuition and aid strategies) is at best a heuristic process.

Recent research indicates that using differentiated prices is potentially a more viable approach to the analysis of pricing alternatives than using net prices. First, studies of the influence of prices and price subsides on persistence indicate that students from different income levels differ in their responses to prices (St. John 1990b; St. John and Starkey *In press*). Second, simulations that used price-response measures that differentiated for income as well as for tuition and different types of student aid proved more accurate than those that used single-standardized coefficients for net price (St. John 1993b). Third, a study that compared alternate ways of specifying the effects of prices—net price (tuition minus grant), net cost (total cost minus total aid), and differentiated prices —on persistence found that the differentiated approach was a substantially better method of predicting persistence (St. John and Starkey *In press*). This research strongly supports the viability of differentiated prices as a more workable approach for integrating price response into budget analyses.

The primary implication of differentiated prices is that this approach provides institutions, state agencies, and the federal government with an improved mechanism for estimating the effects of changes in pricing and an increased capacity to predict the effects of alternative pricing policies, an approach that considers the effects of alternative pricing policies on different populations. Thus, policy analysts can routinely consider the effects of policy alternatives on low-income students and historically underrepresented minorities.

Second, the opportunity for students to make free and informed educational choices is integral to human capital formation. The choices students make about their postsecondary education—whether to attend (access), where to apply and attend (choice of school), and whether to reenroll (persistence)—are the mechanisms through which financing strategies influence enrollment and educational attainment (St. John and Elliott 1994). Thus, the concept of student choice provides an additional basis for public policy decisions about levels of funding, especially when balanced with the emerging construct of return on investment.

This student-choice construct provides a mechanism for linking analyses of the effects of pricing decisions on enrollment with budgetary analyses of the viability of alternative approaches to financing institutions and students. This broad student-choice measure has a historical precedent. Federal student aid programs were created to promote access, college choice, and persistence (Gladieux and Wolanin 1976)—outcomes integral to this broader construct of student choice. Further, when the broader construct is used, it is possible to measure success in achieving gains or losses in student choice in terms of gains or losses in aggregate levels of attainment as well as in attainment by different subpopulations. If this construct were used, national studies of enrollment and persistence could actually be used to assess effects of aid programs on aggregate levels of attainment, potentially improving the link between research on evaluation and policy deliberations. Further, the student-choice construct (and gains or losses in aggregate levels of attainment) can be used in estimates of effects of pricing alternatives, especially when differentiated price-response coefficients are used (e.g., St. John 1993b, 1994a; Trammell 1994).

Third, the process of human capital formation, and especially the fact that substantial tax returns accrue to state and federal investments in higher education (social returns), provide a basis for assessing alternative government financing strategies (social costs). Recent studies strongly indicate that states (Bluestone 1993; Creech, Carpenter, and Davis 1994) and the federal government (St. John and Masten 1990) receive substantial tax revenue returns from government spending on higher education. Further, the new assumption

The opportunity for students to make free and informed educational choices is integral to human capital formation.

that students respond differently to price subsidies than they do to tuition charges creates an opportunity to use returns as a mechanism for assessing alternatives in pricing.

The construct of return on investment provides an alternative to the shorter-term measures of efficiency used by neoconservatives (i.e., default rates). As long as the present value of the tax revenue returns of the public investment in higher education is viewed as a fixed ratio, it does not provide a viable basis for public policy, because it essentially becomes a means of arguing for more resources. Given the new assumptions of differentiated prices, however—that is, that students respond differently to tuition from the way they do to student aid, that students with different backgrounds might respond differently to different types of prices and price subsidies, and that the way students respond to prices can change over time as a result of changes in finance policy—it is possible to develop an approach to return on investment that is more sensitive to changes in policy, including to genuine gains in productivity (expenditures per unit of educational attainment) as contrasted to mere gains in efficiency (expenditures per FTE), which have become a focus of federal and state policy.

Clearly, further analyses would be needed to construct this type of productivity measure. The use of the aggregate measures of postsecondary educational attainment, however, provides a more workable measure than costs per degree (see, e.g., To 1987). As discussed earlier, a long-term measure, such as the costs of producing a degree, would need to be balanced by a short-term measure, such as expenditures per student (Brinkman and Jones 1987). A measure of productivity that focuses on attainment, if properly constructed, could incorporate short-term and long-term measures (e.g., credit hours produced and degrees produced). Further, it would shift the focus of short-term measures from enrollment to credit or course completion, which is a more appropriate measure of productivity.

Fourth, the individual and social costs of human capital formation can be positively influenced by improvements in productivity. Specifically, three types of improvement in productivity can be distinguished:

- *Marginal improvements in productivity.* Reductions in costs that do not substantially change educational outcomes (i.e., cost improvements as a result of changes in class size, teaching loads, and so on);

- *Meaningful changes in productivity.* Gains in the student choice (educational attainment) side of the productivity equation, which can be achieved through new educational practices that improve retention and learning outcomes;
- *Deceptive gains in productivity.* Reductions in the cost side of the productivity equation that influence declines in attainment, which can be caused by inappropriate reductions in cost. (Deceptive productivity could result in lower expenditures per student.)

Both marginal and meaningful improvements in productivity can reduce the individual and social costs of educational attainment (improve affordability for students and taxpayers). To build an understanding of how such improvements can be achieved without falling into the trap of inducing false gains in productivity, however, it is necessary to consider the incentive structures within colleges and universities.

Economic incentives

Understanding 2. *The incentive structure within higher education influences academic and administrative productivity.*

Given that human capital theory does not explicitly contend with economic behavior within organizations, one obviously must step beyond these conceptual boundaries. Based on the review of the literature, two additional considerations related to the internal incentive structure in higher education can make this adjustment to the human capital construct.

First, the incentive for institutions to maximize revenues in their pursuit of excellence needs to be taken into account when government financial strategies are designed and assessed. Given that the apparent validity of the basic precepts of revenue theory held when critically examined, the propensity for institutions to maximize revenues merits routine consideration in policy studies of public finance. This construct has different interpretive meanings at the federal, state, and institutional levels, however.

When considering federal involvement in a policy discourse about productivity in higher education, one must also consider the legitimacy of such a role. First, the federal government's primary role in the financing of higher education is student financial aid. Therefore, the "productivity" of federal student aid programs, as measured by rate of return on investment (gains in student choice [units of attainment] per the amount of revenues expended), should be the major concern at this level. Beyond this issue, which is explored in more depth in the next section, the federal government might not have a legitimate direct role in the political debates over productivity. Rather, efforts to generate information on institutional "waste, fraud, and abuse" in the 1980s appear to have been a diversion from the fact that changes in federal policy influenced declines in minorities' participation rates during that period.

A potential federal role exists, however, in promoting research and productivity—"potential" because the attempts to prove institutions were wasteful did little to build an understanding about how states and institutions could improve their productivity. To a limited extent, the federal government has exercised this role through the Fund for the Improvement of Postsecondary Education, which has included the improvement of productivity in its annual agenda. More generally, numerous topics related to productivity in academe merit further investigation—especially research and development projects aimed at building an understanding of strategies that promote meaningful gains in productivity—and could be supported by federal grants.

States have a direct stake in the policy discourse about productivity in higher education, given their role in funding public institutions. Therefore, the tendency for institutions to maximize revenues is potentially problematic for states. At a minimum, it suggests that states might need a better basis for establishing institutional appropriations than historical practices. Along these lines, peer cost studies, which have been well developed (Brinkman and Teeters 1987), merit consideration. The efforts to establish expenditure targets in Kansas and Minnesota merit review by other states (St. John 1991a). Once appropriate expenditure targets have been established, states are faced with assessing the trade-offs between the viability of institutional and student subsidies. On another level, states should also be concerned about finding ways of fostering marginal and meaningful gains in productivity.

Second, better mechanisms are needed to deal with the incentive structures of faculty and administrators in the distribution and redistribution of resources. Neither human capital theory nor the revenue theory considered how the incentive structures of administrators and faculty influence economic behavior within colleges and universities. The incentives for both faculty and administrators are directly related to their own self and professional interests, influencing the incremental growth in expenditures. Given the current status of public discontent with what is perceived to be excessive expenditures in higher education, it could become more difficult to ignore issues related to productivity, the historic practice. Three generic forces can mitigate these tendencies.

One possibility is that market forces will influence gains in productivity. Over the long term, real (inflation-adjusted) tuition charges, like other revenue sources, have oscillated. Theoretically, market forces—the underlying forces of supply and demand—can influence self-corrections in production costs and prices. The problem is that during the past 15 years, a period when such a correction could have taken place because of the decline in traditional college-age students, neither prices nor the costs of production declined. Indeed, recent analyses indicate that market forces fueled increases in production costs (Getz and Siegfried 1991; Winston 1994). Other forces, including the incentive structure facing faculty and administrators (Winston 1994), mitigated the influence of declining demand on production costs and prices.

A second possibility is that the imposition of external controls will influence gains in productivity. When internal behaviors of professional groups influence costs to rise higher than consumers can afford, government can take steps to implement controls on prices, production costs, or both. These conditions are currently evident in health care (Califano 1994) as well as higher education. In higher education, the federal government began efforts to control costs of production and mitigate price increases through more restrictive regulations on student aid in the 1980s. More recently, several states have begun to consider or implement regulatory constraints aimed at reducing costs. Unfortunately, such strategies appear to lead to false gains in productivity—reductions in cost that decrease students' choices, educational attainment, and other outcomes.

A third untried alternative is to increase empowerment and responsibility. A few authors have proposed that increases in professional responsibility are a potential means of controlling production costs in higher education. In particular, a proposal to use action-oriented inquiry—experiments designed by faculty and administrators—as a means of discovering ways of simultaneously reducing production costs and improving quality merits further exploration (Levin 1991). Such developments could have potential if they are coupled with reforms in governance that "empower" by increasing the professional responsibility of faculty and administrators. In combination, the process of reforming governance and using action-oriented inquiry is characterized as "empowerment coupled with responsibility," a term derived from the literature on accelerated schools (Hopfenberg, Levin, and Associates 1993; Levin 1986, 1987).

Higher education is currently enmeshed in political debates about controls. These political debates hold the threat of imposing more external controls and restrictions on higher education, but those actions could have the unintended effect of actually raising costs. For example, the pending requirement to have all postsecondary institutions annually report their retention rates and the placement of their graduates, a policy developed to inform consumers about quality, will probably influence production costs to increase, given the added costs of generating reports about the placement of graduates. Further, many states are imposing tighter controls on public higher education, which could restrict faculty members' freedoms and increase teaching contact hours, changes that could reduce student choice (and promote false gains in productivity). The alternative of trying to empower faculty and administrators to take more professional responsibility merits exploration, and two specific issues merit consideration in the design of such strategies.

1. The incentives for administrators, which are to build large programs and staffs and to increase their administrative portfolios, are a set of behaviors that are generally rewarded with higher pay. When these incentives are not adequately mitigated by other forces, administrators build empires, a phenomenon frequently referred to as the "administrative lattice" (Knutsen 1993; Massy and Wilger 1992; Massy and Zemsky 1992). Regardless of the perspective one holds on this phenomenon, some means of constraining costs is needed. Recent efforts by the National Association of College and University Business Officers to reward administrators who initiate cost-saving

measures illustrate that it is possible to engage administrators in inquiry and experimentation along these lines when workable incentives are evident.

2. The primary incentive for faculty is to pursue professional development in their areas of interest, including the personal freedom to conduct research and create programs with professional colleagues. Most basic research is conducted by faculty in doctoral and research universities, however. Therefore, the possibility exists that faculty involvement in action research aimed at improving learning processes while constraining costs (meaningful productivity) could become a means of enhancing the professionalization of faculty in other types of institutions (especially in comprehensive colleges and community colleges), providing appropriate incentives for such activities are established (St. John 1994b).

An incremental process
Understanding 3. *Policy studies on higher education finance are appropriately conceived as mechanisms for informing incremental policy decisions.*

The past 15 years of rising tuitions and declining government support illustrate that higher education policy responds to conditions as they develop rather than to plans developed using systematic and rational methodologies. Therefore, administrators and analysts at all levels of policy making are bound to encounter frustrations if they assume that comprehensive and systematic analyses can have a sustaining effect on policy deliberations. Two considerations can affect the design of policy studies aimed at informing incremental policy decisions.

First, because unanticipated conditions will undermine even the best-designed systematic reforms, more emphasis should be given to policy studies and analytic approaches that can inform incremental decisions. Despite the advent of master planning (Halstead 1974), few states have followed systematic plans for the development of state systems of higher education. And while states with strong centralized control of their higher education systems might be more effective at initiating reforms, such as the implementation of assessment processes (Hearn and Griswold 1994), centralized authority does not positively influence institutional quality

(Volkwein 1989). Further, even systematic federal reforms, such as the creation of federal student aid programs under the Higher Education Act of 1965 or the Education Amendments of 1972, are subject to substantial revisions through annual budgetary and legislative processes (Hearn 1993). Thus, planning and evaluation studies with long-term horizons should consider the volatility of policy making over the long term.

More important, greater attention needs to be given to the design and conduct of analytic studies that can inform incremental policy decisions. Two domains of institutional decisions are germane. First, boards and administrators in colleges and universities are concerned about generating revenues. Along these lines, annual decisions about tuition and aid strategies and external economic conditions are crucial.

Second, efforts should be made to promote a culture in colleges and universities that supports action inquiry. Since Dewey, educators have speculated about the use of inquiry in refining educational processes. The ideal of using inquiry to inform and transform practice is as applicable to higher education as it is to elementary and secondary education. Generally, inquiry involves:

- *Building an understanding of the challenge.* Brainstorming about why the problem exists, generating hypotheses about the causes of the problem, and testing those hypotheses through formal or informal research.
- *Identifying possible solutions.* Looking externally to other colleges and universities to find experiments that have been tried, looking internally to see how others have contended with the challenges, and thinking creatively about new possibilities.
- *Synthesizing solutions into an action plan.* Assessing the possible solutions relative to the understanding of the challenge (the results of hypothesis testing) and developing a plan that considers time horizons, resource requirements and acquisitions, pilot test strategies, and evaluation strategies.
- *Pilot testing solutions.* Approaching the "trying out" of new ideas as action experiments. A fundamental problem with conventional planning and budgeting in higher education, including the process of proposing and implementing curricula, is that it is usually assumed that the selected

solutions will work. Evidence to the contrary is generally ignored. If new solutions are treated as pilot tests by those who implement them, then they have an opportunity to evolve their practice—that is, to develop as reflective practitioners.

* *Evaluating and refining.* Assessing whether the solution has actually addressed the challenge, assessing how the new practice can be tried and improved, using the results to feed back into the evolving understanding of the challenge (closing the loop), and making decisions about the continuation and refinement of the practice.

Such an action inquiry (adapted from Brunner and Hopfenberg *In press*)—one that links investigations into challenge areas with the assessment of action experiments—could be essential to the revitalization of both academic and administrative departments. Given the issues addressed in this study, an inquiry-based approach appears applicable to a wide range of related issues, including the crucial issues of productivity (academic and administrative) and pricing (at all levels).

The political economy

Understanding 4. *Policy studies on higher education finance should routinely consider both political and economic influences on resource allocations.*

It is evident from the review of changes in federal, state, and institutional financial strategies that the various influences of political and economic forces are not routinely considered, yet these forces substantially influence policy deliberations. Further, social inequities increased as a result of incremental policy decisions made during the past 15 years. Two issues merit consideration in the design, execution, and interpretation of policy studies.

First, analyses of institutional, state, and federal financing decisions should routinely consider the direct effects on student choice, especially the opportunity for minorities to complete college. For the past decade, most state and federal financial policies ignored the influence of incremental appropriations on the enrollment of minorities. As has been discussed previously and elaborated on elsewhere (Kaltenbaugh 1993; St. John 1991d), these policies limited opportunities for some students, especially African-Americans. The reconstructed approach to assessing the effects of prices and price subsidies on human capital formation provides a potential mechanism for assessing the effects of current and future policies on equal opportunities.

Second, better mechanisms are needed to involve diverse faculty in processes that distribute and redistribute resources. External political forces affect the power of some internal groups to influence the allocation of resources. During the 1980s, for example, faculty in engineering, business, and computer science realized larger average pay increases than faculty in other fields (Kirshstein, Tikoff, et al. 1990). While the power of faculty from some disciplines to command higher salaries is a commonly accepted manifestation of the political power of some highly prestigious fields, the fact that these same power relations can strongly influence the redistribution of resources in periods of retrenchment has only recently been illuminated (Gumport 1993; Slaughter 1993a, 1993b). This more recent research raises serious questions about the influence of political and economic power on planning and budgeting.

In fact, the unequal power relations within academic communities are perplexing problems for which no easy solutions exist (Slaughter 1993a). Part of the problem is that budget planning and resource allocation has historically been a centralized process in higher education, with faculty committees serving in an "advisory role" (American Association 1966). Membership on these advisory committees has been influenced by the ability to attract external resources, among other power-related factors (Pfeffer and Moore 1980), and programs that have historically served women and minorities have lacked this political power (Slaughter 1993a). Thus, the mechanisms used to plan for the distribution of resources have historically favored faculty from departments that attract high levels of external resources.

An alternative that has been seldom tried is to delegate budget authority, to allow certain portions of tuition and other revenues (state appropriations) to follow students to departments. For example, responsibilities for setting tuition and salaries and for allocating positions could be delegated. The technical mechanisms for such a process have long been available (e.g., the Induced Course Load Matrix and the Resource Requirement Planning Model), and the logical structure of these models is easy to develop using computerized spread sheets. Such a decentralization is highly compatible with the concept of empowerment coupled with responsibility and merits experimentation. Such mechanisms, however, could infringe on institutional autonomy, as it has traditionally been framed in the literature on state policy (Hearn and Griswold 1994).

Intermediate Reflections

Building an understanding of the consequences of financial strategies is a recursive process, with gains in understanding emerging from reflection on experience. Untested theoretical assumptions and ideological beliefs can hinder the process, as was the case in the 1980s, when the basic assumptions used to guide financial strategy in higher education metamorphosed. Before the 1980s, a relatively static set of theories (e.g., human capital theory) and ideologies (conventional liberal and conservative values, both of which shared progressive assumptions but disagreed on the mechanism for promoting progress) was commonly held in the higher education community and society. In the 1980s, more divergent theories and ideologies emerged and new practices developed, creating a new opportunity for reflection and redirection.

This section is an initial attempt to build a new, intermediate understanding of how colleges and government agencies might systematically examine financial conditions and strategies. The understandings reached here can no doubt be further refined based on research and experience with new approaches to higher education finance. Thus, these guiding principles represent a basis for assessing alternative financial strategies and therefore provide a potentially "workable" reconstruction of theory. These new theoretical claims merit further critical review, however.

ASSESSING FINANCIAL STRATEGIES

Two general lessons can be derived from this review. First, any single policy solution carries with it a set of consequences that can be only partially anticipated. By opening the practical process of making policy choices to a wider range of possibilities, it could be possible to make more informed choices. Second, because it is not possible to anticipate all the consequences of major policy choices, it is important that means be created to assess the consequences of incremental policy changes so that the course of policy can be adjusted. Therefore, when assessing alternative strategies for contending with the emerging crisis in college costs, it is necessary to consider strategies that modify the systemic process—the systems and procedures used to govern higher education—as well as strategies that can be used in the incremental policy process in which budgets and programs are changed. This section uses the reconstructed finance framework to assess, in a preliminary way, a range of approaches to financial strategy that could be used by the federal government, states, and institutions to contend with the emerging cost issues.

The opportunity to enroll in a four-year college was reduced for students from the poorest backgrounds as a result of the restructuring of federal programs.

Assessing Federal Strategies
Financial aid is the primary federal role in the financing of higher education. The evidence reviewed here indicates that federal student aid is potentially effective in promoting educational opportunity for low-income students and educational choice for middle-income students. In the 1980s, the opportunity to enroll in a four-year college was reduced for students from the poorest backgrounds as a result of the restructuring of federal programs. Middle-income students still had a choice, however, because they responded more positively to loans. Given the erosion in opportunity for poor students, several individuals and groups have undertaken efforts to redesign federal student aid programs. Most of the literature on financial strategy in higher education focuses on making major systemic reforms to the programs rather than on the consequences of incremental policy decisions. The framework developed in the previous section is used in the following paragraphs to examine a few recently proposed systemic reforms as well as to suggest strategies that could be used to refine the incremental policy process.

Systemic reforms
Table 6 assesses three alternatives discussed in the recent literature on higher education, using the reconstructed finance

TABLE 6

A PRELIMINARY ASSESSMENT OF SYSTEMIC REFORMS IN FEDERAL STUDENT AID

Option	Choice (Attainment)	Role of Return on Investment	Costs	Risks
Status quo				
Title IV programs subject to budget	Provides opportunity for poor to attend and choice for middle-income students	Approximately $4.30 tax revenue return per dollar spent	Approximately $14.5 billion per year (FY1990)	Budget and other constraints reduce opportunity
Alternative approaches				
• Award Even Start grants (Haveman 1988)	Substantial increase in opportunity and choice	Substantial reduction in returns, as many recipients will make other choices	Substantial increase as a result of universal grant awards	Extremely difficult strategy to sustain
• Treat Pell as entitlement and implement federal packaging (National Commission on Responsibilities 1993)	Moderate improvements in opportunity and choice because of the stable structure	Very little change, as the basic structure of Title IV programs does not change	Moderate increase as a result of full funding of Title IV programs	Less risk for students; could be little support for entitlement provisions
• Restructure federal programs to promote high tuition/high aid in states (Congressional Budget Office 1991)	Moderate gains as a result of improved opportunity in public higher education	Moderate decline in federal returns, because federal dollars would increase	Moderate to substantial, depending on cost provisions	Difficult to maintain political support because of reduced returns

framework. This preliminary look at the likely effects of these changes considers the effects on student choice (and attainment) and the rate of tax return on investment. The assessment uses recent analyses of students' responses to price (St. John 1990a, 1990b, 1993b, 1994a) and the return on the federal investment in student aid (St. John and Masten 1990) to estimate the likely direction (but not the extent) of the effects.

The first proposal examined would replace federal student aid and other federal training programs with a new Even Start grant of $20,000 for each college-age youth (Haveman 1988). The grant could be used for education, health, housing, or investment opportunities. The preliminary assessment of this option indicates that the proposal would increase students' choice and opportunity but would probably reduce the returns ratios compared to the student aid programs it would replace, as the Even Start grants could be used for other purposes. Further, the costs of the Even Start grants would be substantially more than the current student aid programs they would replace, because more individuals would receive subsidies (the entire college-age population) and the subsidies would be substantially greater than the amount the average aid recipient now receives during his or her college years.

Second, a recently developed set of proposals for stabilizing the federal role in student aid (National Commission on Responsibilities 1993) includes full implementation of the provisions in Title IV grant programs by requiring full funding along with a federal strategy to ensure a consistent approach to packaging. The new plan would result in improved choice for both low- and middle-income students, because the provisions appear sufficient to compensate for the marginal changes in institutional tuition over the past decade. Further, it is anticipated that this proposal would maintain the current return on the federal investment in student aid, estimated to be about $4.30 per dollar spent (St. John and Masten 1990). The provisions for entitlement would reduce the risks associated with responding to budget constraints by cutting federal student aid programs. Such a strategy might receive some political support, given that the Clinton administration has proposed full funding of the Pell program (Zook 1994a).

The third strategy, restructuring student aid to promote a shift in state financing from institutional subsidies to student subsidies (Congressional Budget Office 1991), could result in modest gains in opportunity if it is adequately and consistently funded at both the state and federal levels. Given the recent record of state (Hines 1988, 1993) and federal governments on funding higher education, however, this proposition is questionable. Further, the strategy would actually reduce the returns ratio on the federal investment, because some federal dollars would be used to replace state dollars, assuming a financial incentive would be given to states for changing their financial strategies. These proposals that the federal government take steps to stimulate privatization (e.g., Congressional Budget Office 1991; Fischer 1990) are not necessarily in the federal interest and are more appropriately viewed as state strategies. Thus, of these three strategies, the one from the National Commission on Responsibilities for Financing Postsecondary Education seems to come the closest to remedying the problems created by changes in the federal role during the past two decades. It is interesting to note, however, that none of the proposals reviewed would actually improve the rate of tax revenue returns on the federal investment.

The U.S. Department of Education recently announced a set of proposed changes in the Title IV student aid program that are intended to make them a better "investment," including the elimination of Pell funding for college students in developmental education (Zook 1994c). According to the reconstructed framework, one would need to assess the long-term effects of the proposed changes on educational attainment, tax revenues, and costs of other social programs before being able to tell whether these strategies are really sound investment decisions. Based on a surface scan of these proposals, however, it appears that they will eliminate some of the highest-risk students, which could mean that these actions could increase the costs of other programs, given that adults in at-risk situations are more likely to cost taxpayers money from other programs if they do not acquire sufficient skills to seek employment. Therefore, the reconstructed framework potentially provides a broader and more complete lens for assessing these policy proposals.

Incremental changes

The incremental process of changing programs and developing program budgets could be more important than the meta-analysis of aid policies and the assessment of proposals for systemic reforms. Three practical suggestions address the enhancement of analytic strategies to assess incremental policy changes.

First, shifting from the net-price approach to differentiated prices could improve the capacity of budget models to predict the effects of changes in aid policy. Adhering to the concept of net price has foiled previous efforts to integrate price-response measures into federal budget models. After development of a procedure for using price-response measures using a single standardized measure (National Commission on the Financing 1973), several attempts were made to improve the methods used to calculate price-response measures (Jackson and Weathersby 1975; Leslie and Brinkman 1988; McPherson 1978), but these efforts carried forward the net-price assumption. A recent study that compared the use of net-price measures to the use of measures that differentiate for both income and the type of aid under consideration (grants, loans, and work) found that the use of net-price measures was much less accurate than the use of trends to project enrollment but that the differentiated approach was about as accurate at projects that used trends but also showed the redistributional effects of price changes on enrollment across sectors (St. John 1993b). Thus, the use of differentiated measures has the potential of overcoming the long-held problems with models that attempt to estimate the effects of prices on enrollment; they are not accurate enough to have even a heuristic value (Dresch 1975). The newer approaches appear to overcome this obstacle. Therefore, the methods used to assess the effects of budget proposals for federal student aid could be refined to provide insight into the effects of various budget proposals on the enrollment behavior of low-income and middle-income populations.

Second, more effort should be made to communicate through public media the results of budget analyses. Unfortunately, the popular press continually demonstrates very little understanding of the social consequences of budgetary decisions in higher education. The popular press has been conditioned to react negatively to the costs of student aid programs but has infrequently been provided information on, or insight into, the consequences of the various choices being made. Given the critical influence of the annual budget process on participation rates for minorities and low-income students, this situation is highly problematic. The reconstructed financial framework provides a potential basis for estimating these effects.

Third, more attention should be given to assessing the effects of incremental changes in program funding and regulations. A brief examination of recent federal efforts to limit eligibility for federal loan programs by schools with high default rates (e.g., Zook 1993) is used here to illustrate how this question might be approached. Unfortunately, the potential effects of these new policies were not systematically examined. A recent case study of a proprietary school with a low default rate illustrates how the regulations themselves can create the problems they intend to resolve (Peterson 1994). While the school studied, a beauty school, had low default rates, it took the initiative to discourage loans to minimize future risk when the new regulations were developed. The Title IV regulations, however, prevented the school from refusing GSL (guaranteed student loan) students who had arranged their own loans through participating lenders. As a consequence of these two developments, the percentage of the total student body in the school who had loans declined, but the percentage of loans that were in default climbed substantially (increasing from less than 10 percent to more than 50 percent in two years), increasing its risk of losing Title IV funds. The school voluntarily withdrew from the GSL program. Other research indicates that the receipt of student aid is positively associated with persistence in proprietary schools (St. John, et al. *In press*) and that defaults are influenced by students' background but not by institutional loan practices (Wilms, Moore, and Bolus 1987). While some recent research indicates that the earnings differentials for graduates of proprietary schools and high schools might not be sufficient to justify the use of loans (Grubb 1993, 1994), proprietary education could still be a worthwhile public investment. For example, many proprietary students are not high school graduates and could cost taxpayers an amount for social welfare if they did not have an opportunity for postsecondary training (St. John, et al. *In press*); further, other gains in productivity could accrue from this investment (see, e.g., Paulsen 1994). Based on these considerations, it would appear that regulatory processes that eliminate eligibility for Title IV for institutions with high default rates would result in a decrease in choice (and attainment) as a result of a reduction in opportunities in postsecondary schools and colleges that have historically served low-income students. They might also reduce the rate of return, given that the high-risk students who attend community colleges and proprietary schools are those who have the highest potential tax revenue returns to the federal government, despite their higher probability of default. If these high-risk students do not get postsecondary training, then they are far more likely to cost taxpayers through social welfare programs. Thus, the returns ratio for this population could be much greater than for the average aid recipient.

While these assessments are preliminary, they illustrate that the reconstructed financial framework can be used to assess alternative program changes and to communicate about them with the public. At the very least, this example illustrates that the incremental budgetary and regulatory processes influence the effectiveness of student aid programs. Analysts working for the U.S. Department of Education and its contractors, and national associations that routinely comment on proposed federal regulations could potentially use the reconstructed financial framework. Such analyses could provide a basis for communicating with postsecondary institutions and the public the current approach to regulatory change.

Assessing State Strategies

Most of the literature on the states' role in higher education focuses on the states' role in planning and coordination (Hines 1988; Mingle 1988b; Volkwein 1987) and on the financing of higher education. The evidence reviewed in this study supports the arguments that states' financing decisions influenced the increases in tuition during the past decade and a half, that these developments adversely affected enrollment of low-income and minority students, and that states have a poor record of managing costs in higher education. This subsection suggests strategies states can use to improve these outcomes, using the framework developed in the previous section.

The framework provides three criteria that can be used to assess the likely effects of systemic reforms and incremental policy changes: *the potential for improving productivity,* distinguishing marginal, meaningful, and deceptive gains in productivity as measured by the ratio of expenditures per unit of attainment; *student choice,* using the differentiated price-response concept to assess the effects of price changes on attainment as measured by credit-hour production and/or degrees produced; and *return on investment,* using a ratio of expenditures for higher education compared to the net present value of future tax revenue returns attributable to the gains in attainment attributable to the investment. The following paragraphs illustrate how these criteria can be used to assess a range of systemic and incremental policy changes. Again, the preliminary assessments consider the likely direction of change, but no attempt was made here to estimate actual enrollments or costs of specific policy options.

Systemic reforms

Two types of systemic reforms—privatization and high tuition/high grant aid—are examined briefly in the following paragraphs, using the reconstructed financial framework. Both of these alternatives have been proposed from time to time as means of reducing state taxpayers' costs.

In the midst of the current wave of cutbacks in state appropriations to higher education, some observers have speculated about the prospect of privatizing public higher education (see, e.g., Congressional Budget Office 1991; Creech, Carpenter, and Davis 1994). This alternative could involve decreasing state control and appropriations, possibly with some commitment for most levels of state appropriations and/or student grants. When the reconstructed financial framework is used to examine this alternative, the benefits of making this shift are suspect.

First, privatization of public higher education would weaken states' capacity to influence productivity, as the links between state action and institutional financial practices would essentially be eliminated. Privatization would essentially eliminate the states' role in financing institutions and coordinating academic programs, leaving productivity to be influenced entirely by market forces. Given that the incentive structure within higher education provides few direct incentives for instructional productivity, there is reason to doubt whether privatization would lead to meaningful gains in productivity. Instead, it is possible that reductions in state appropriations would result in substantial increases in tuition, which could also decrease enrollments. It is likely that such a sequence of events would actually increase expenditures per student, a conclusion based on research that indicates that expenditures per student are likely to rise when enrollments drop (Getz and Siegfried 1991).

Second, the privatization of public higher education is likely to result in dramatically reduced choices (and attainment) for students, unless states make a substantial commitment of need-based grants. Analyses of the effects of tuition charges on persistence (St. John, Oescher, and Andrieu 1992) and of changes in tuition charges on enrollment (St. John 1993b, 1994a) indicate that substantial increases in tuition charges decreased enrollments, especially when they were not linked to increases in tuition.

Third, privatization could slightly improve the ratio of return on states' investment to the extent that grant strategies are used; however, substantial losses would occur in productivity of the workforce unless a substantial amount were spent on student grants. Research indicates that student aid dollars have a higher rate of return than state appropriations (and tuition). Thus, to the extent that privatization is coupled with a state's commitment to need-based student aid, the overall ratio would improve. To the extent that student choice (and postsecondary attainment) is reduced, however, one can anticipate a reduction in productivity of the workforce (Paulsen 1994). In sum, the privatization of public higher education appears highly problematic.

The high-tuition, high-aid strategy has often been advocated as an alternative to the incremental erosion of state appropriations to institutions without an increased commitment to student aid (e.g., Hearn and Longanecker 1985; McPherson and Schapiro 1991; Wallace 1992). The critical feature of this strategy is ensuring the link between increases in tuition (reductions in appropriations) and increases in aid (Griswold and Marine *In press*). The preliminary assessment indicates that high tuition/high aid has substantial advantages for states, especially when compared to the current practice of increasing tuition without increasing state grants.

First, high tuition/high aid would have little direct influence on levels of productivity in public colleges and universities, because the high-tuition, high-aid strategy essentially shifts a portion of the burden for financing public higher education from taxpayers to students and their families without substantially influencing the basic cost structures within colleges and universities.

Second, high tuition/high aid essentially maintains students' choice (and attainment) while reducing taxpayers' costs. Recent studies indicate that students are more responsive to grant dollars than tuition dollars in their decisions about first-time enrollment and persistence (St. John 1990a, 1990b). Thus, fall enrollments would be maintained reasonably well under a high-tuition, high-aid strategy. Tuition is negatively associated with within-year persistence, however (St. John et al. 1994; St. John, Oescher, and Andrieu 1992; St. John and Starkey *In press*), and the time it takes to attain a degree could therefore be increased slightly in states that use this strategy.

Third, high tuition/high aid improves the rate of return for tax revenue on the public investment in higher education. Analyses of the return on states' investment in higher education focus on appropriations to institutions rather than to student aid (Bluestone 1993; Creech, Carpenter, and Davis 1994; Girling, Goldman, and Keith 1993). These studies therefore provide little insight into whether shifts to a high-tuition, high-aid strategy would influence a change in the rate of return. Given the national research on the effects of prices and price subsidies (McPherson and Schapiro 1991; St. John

1990a, 1990b) and the research on the high-tuition, high-aid strategy in Minnesota (Hearn and Anderson 1989), however, substantial reason exists to expect that the rate of return on the state investment would improve substantially.

Incremental changes

The review of the literature on state financial strategies indicates that the pattern of change in state policy had two problematic aspects: Incremental changes in pricing have negatively influenced opportunity for students, especially for low-income students; and states have a poor record in cost management. The reconstructed financial framework can be used to inform incremental policy choices in both areas.

Improving productivity. Historically, most states have funded institutions better when they have had sufficient tax revenues than when shortfalls occurred. In this environment of feast or famine, states have generally lacked mechanisms for controlling cost structures within higher education, as institutions have tended to substitute tuition revenues for losses in state support in times of financial instability. Thus, states need to balance their historic concerns about the adequacy of spending on public higher education with emerging concerns about efficiency and productivity. If these perspectives are both deemed important, in the sense of reconciling opposites, then it might be possible to distinguish marginal, meaningful, and deceptive gains in productivity.

The reconstructed financial framework can be used to conceptualize and assess alternative strategies for improving productivity in higher education, with an emphasis on promoting marginal and meaningful gains but avoiding deceptive gains. Given recent developments in higher education, three types of strategies merit consideration: implementing cost controls, refining management techniques, and changing incentive structures.

First, the imposition of external cost controls, a pattern that has evolved in some states (St. John 1994b), runs the risk of reducing choice (and attainment) for students and the return on public investment as a result of deceptive gains in productivity. Because of the widely held public perception of waste in public higher education, some states have begun to micro-manage faculty teaching loads, salary increases, travel, and other cost mechanisms. In Louisiana, for example, legislation enacted in 1993 (Act 237) created the Louisiana Accountability in Public Higher Education Advisory Committee to study these issues and recommend an appropriate set of controls. When states reduce expenditures per student by limiting salary increases, increasing teaching loads, and limiting faculty capacity to keep current in their fields, they run a strong risk of creating deceptive gains in productivity—a reduction in average expenditures that influences a reduction in student outcomes. When carried to an extreme, these practices could undermine the quality of education, reducing educational attainment and possibly reducing tax revenue returns from the public investment in higher education.

Second, new management practices, such as increased use of cost studies and quality management, can potentially influence marginal, or perhaps even meaningful, gains in productivity. These techniques can be undermined by the incentive structure in higher education and the state political process, however. Some states have begun to deal with the cost crisis by adopting new management techniques. Minnesota and Kansas, for example, have used program cost studies to establish funding targets by field (St. John 1991a). Minnesota established funding targets for high-, middle-, and low-cost fields at the lower-division, upper-division, and graduate levels, then set a goal of funding two-thirds of the target (Berg and Hoenack 1987; St. John 1991a), a technique that enabled the state to link institutional appropriations and increases in tuition to awards in the state grant program. Further, some states have begun to advocate quality management techniques as a means of encouraging public institutions to focus on quality of educational programs and academic services in an environment of declining resources (Chaffee and Sherr 1992; Knutsen 1993). These and other management techniques potentially give states mechanisms for balancing concerns about adequacy of funding and educational outcomes with the emergent concerns about achieving greater economies. Thus, these techniques hold more potential than overt cost-control mechanisms for promoting marginal or meaningful gains in productivity. To the extent that these actions actually influence marginal gains in productivity—real reductions in the costs of educational attainment for students and taxpayers—they will improve the return on the state's investment. Additionally, to the extent that they result in meaningful gains

New management practices can be subverted by the political nature of the state budget process.

in productivity—improvements in educational outcomes per a given level of expenditure—they will result in improvements in students' choice and in the rate of return on taxpayers' investment.

New management practices can be subverted, however, by the political nature of the state budget process (Layzell and Lyddon 1990) and the incentive structure in colleges and universities. State legislators are reelected by meeting the needs of constituents; thus, they have an incentive to promote special support for colleges and universities in their districts. On a practical level, it means that whenever new systems are implemented to control state expenditures, institutions can lobby local legislators for special appropriations. For example, when Minnesota implemented its average-cost funding, most budget line-item appropriations were eliminated, but the number of line items began to grow again after the new funding policy was implemented (St. John 1991a). Similarly, past generations of educational leaders and legislators have found ways to undermine, or topple, other management techniques like management by objective, zero-based budgeting, and strategic planning. Thus, analysts and policy makers who advocate and adopt managerial solutions to the crisis in college costs are faced with the prospect that the intent of their new programs will be undermined over time because of the special interests of various constituencies.

A third alternative, changing the financing incentive structures used in financing public higher education, merits more systematic and serious consideration. Two levels of the incentive structure in particular merit closer scrutiny: the incentives for institutions to maximize state appropriations and the incentives within colleges and universities to maximize revenues in academic and administrative units. The historic financing strategy used by most states, providing funds on the basis of FTE fall enrollment, provided an incentive for institutions to maximize enrollment but not necessarily to improve retention or learning outcomes. An alternative approach developed in Minnesota, funding based on full-year enrollment (Berg and Hoenack 1987; St. John 1991a), partially increases incentives to retain students. Other alternatives that link funding to credit-hour and degree production also merit serious consideration. While on one level such techniques could be perceived as providing an incentive to pass students rather than educate them, over the longer term the freedom of students to choose would probably diminish that type of devaluation of education. Thus, mechanisms that link funding to credit-hour and degree production could provide an incentive for institutions to improve their retention and learning outcomes, and they merit further consideration.

Unfortunately, very little is known about how states can facilitate change in the internal financial incentive structures in higher education. One possibility is for states to fund institutional studies of strategies for improving meaningful improvements in productivity: improvements in learning outcomes and administrative productivity. While this strategy would not change the incentive structure, it would at least help build an understanding of techniques that improve student outcomes.

Additionally, states should consider experimenting with mechanisms that ensure an appropriate flow of funds within public colleges and universities to the programs that produce credit hours and graduates. While there are reasons for states to be cautious about such strategies because they could infringe on institutional autonomy, there are also reasons for such strategies to be explored. Specifically, if state appropriations followed students to programs, then students' choice is enhanced and the negative influence of politically powerful departments and programs would be somewhat mitigated.

Linking tuition and grants. With the erosion in federal Pell grants and the increase in public sector tuition, it is critical that states develop better ways of linking tuition and student grants. A recent study indicates that when a family's ability to pay is taken into account, Pell grants have become a regressive program—that Pell recipients actually have a greater burden than nonrecipients (Minnesota Higher Education 1994). Further, an adequately funded need-based grant program can create a more progressive environment.

For states to provide access for all students, they need to develop mechanisms that link appropriate increases in grant programs to increases in tuition. In recent years, the methods states can use to analyze alternative approaches to state grants (Setter and Rayburn 1994), evaluate the effects of grant programs (St. John 1992b; Somers and St. John 1993), and assess alternative financing strategies (Hearn and Longanecker 1985; St. John 1993b, 1994a) have been improved. These tools can help states design better programs, although it has proven quite difficult for states to maintain a link between grants and tuition (Griswold and Marine *In press*).

Assessing Institutional Strategies

The crisis in college costs presents a new set of financial problems for colleges and universities. In the mid-1990s, college costs have risen to a point beyond the willingness of taxpayers to support higher education and the ability of most students to pay the costs of attending. The financial strategy used during the past 15 years—raising tuition to compensate for losses in state appropriations and federal grants and to fund enhancements to academic programs and student services—has resulted in a price spiral that has placed the full cost of attending beyond the means of the majority of students. This subsection assesses a range of systemic reforms and incremental changes relative to their ability to improve productivity and affordability. Then, based on this analysis, it proposes a systematic approach to restructuring—an approach that focuses on transforming both financial and academic strategies as a means of improving affordability and productivity.

Systemic reforms

Given the ways colleges and universities have responded to previous financial crises, three types of systemic reforms merit their consideration: implementation of cost controls, development of new managerial approaches, and changes in the incentive structure.

First, while the imposition of cost controls can reduce short-term production costs and thus provide a means of adjusting to short-term revenue losses, it can drive up the long-term costs of higher education for students and taxpayers. When confronted by within-year reductions in revenues, colleges and universities typically respond by reducing variable costs—telephones, travel, other operating costs, part-time instructors, and unclassified employees. When constraints on revenues are sustained over a longer period, institutions tend to respond by holding salaries down, not filling faculty and staff positions when they open, and reducing basic costs by other means. This type of erosion can impair the quality of instruction, reduce offerings, and decrease completion rates, either as the result of rising charges or the lack of courses available. Therefore, the implementation of cost controls would appear to be the least desirable means of responding to the crisis in college costs, as it can lead to deceptive gains in productivity.

Second, the development of refined managerial techniques provides a potential means of responding to the crisis in college costs by making marginal improvements in productivity and sound pricing decisions (on tuition and student aid), at least in the short term. For example, the strategy proposed by the U.S. Department of Education in *Tough Choices* (ca. 1990) is for a centralized committee to guide a strategic process that combines an emphasis on quality outcomes and services with a concern about costs. A similar strategy, emphasizing the integration of quality management techniques, has been proposed in California as a way of dealing with reduced state appropriations (Knutsen 1993). Further, a range of recently proposed quality management strategies (Chaffee and Sherr 1992; Seymour 1993; Sherr and Teeter 1991) can be used to address quality and productivity (Sloan 1994). And an emphasis on productivity can be integrated into strategic planning, which generally includes an emphasis on having a central steering committee and strong presidential leadership (e.g., Brown 1988; Cyert 1988; Foote 1988; Lisensky 1988; Swain 1988). A continuation of current trends toward public dissatisfaction with the costs of public higher education could influence many institutions, especially in the public sector, to integrate these processes into existing strategic planning and management processes. To the extent that these managerial innovations get policy makers to engage in a proactive approach to dealing with issues of productivity, they would probably increase the ability of institutions to respond to new financial conditions. Managerial changes have some major limitations, however.

Managerial changes aimed at reducing operating costs can easily be undermined by experienced and powerful constituents, which could lessen their ability to reduce these costs. Higher education has a long history of developing new managerial practices that were designed to control costs. The first wave of systemic reforms (see, e.g., Weathersby and Balderston 1971, 1972) failed because they were too cumbersome. The second wave, started in response to the "new depression" (Balderston 1974; Cheit 1971, 1973), has changed management practices and helped institutions to adapt to changing conditions but only temporarily mitigated escalating operating costs; that is, educational and related expenditures per student did not rise in the early 1970s as fast as inflation (Kirshstein, Tikoff, et al. 1990). And the third wave, the strategic revolution (Chaffee 1984, 1985, 1989; Keller 1983; Steeples 1988a), apparently hastened the rise in educational expenditures and tuition in the 1980s. The problem is that these managerial innovations do very little to change the internal incentive structures in colleges and universities.

Further, the centralized nature of managerial innovations circumvents the equalizing aspects of governance, which means they have a tendency to favor programs that serve elite professions. One "successful" strategic planning process "progressed in strict secrecy, for premature disclosure carried two risks[, one of which] was that the faculty might force prolonged debate of any proposal . . ." (Steeples 1988a, p. 76). The fact is that most "strategic" processes create centralized committees that get around the characteristically cumbersome and ineffectual faculty governance structure (Keller 1983; Norris and Poulton 1987; Steeples 1988a). The problem is that the centralized committees that are formed to "steer" strategic planning usually include heavier representation from politically powerful departments (see, e.g., Pfeffer and Moore 1980), increasing the influence of their interests on the process. The result of these inequities in the distribution, redistribution, and reduction of resources is that middle-class and female-dominated majors are usually the hardest hit (St. John 1993a; Slaughter 1993a).

Third, the alternative of adapting the incentive structure in colleges and universities merits consideration, because these strategies could hold the greatest potential for reducing excesses and making college more affordable. Historically, colleges and universities maintained separate authority structures for academic and financial decisions: Faculty had greater influence on educational policies and plans, administrators and trustees more influence on the acquisition and distribution of resources. Because one set of decisions was decentralized and the other centralized, a form of often troublesome gridlock occurred, and the checks and balances might have created incentives to be unproductive. Strategic methodologies circumvented this situation by centralizing the major educational and financial decisions and coordinating the two processes, but they did little to change the internal incentive structure. Rather, they created opportunities for powerful faculty and departments to use the process to generate more revenues. An alternative approach might be to delegate responsibility for both educational and financial decisions. Doing so would give academic units more responsibility for setting their own prices (tuition and aid), salaries, hiring practices, and contingencies for retrenchment. Tuition revenues and state appropriations would need to "follow" students to departmental budgets. Then faculty would be responsible for cutting their own budgets when necessary. Indeed, academic departments would be responsible for their own finances.

Those choosing such a strategy need to proceed with caution—through deliberate pilot testing—to ensure that students' and taxpayers' interests are represented in the process. Such changes in the basic financial structure have a potential to improve the underlying inequity of university budgets. The departments that have been cash cows—having had their revenues milked to support the elite, high-cost fields—would be on more equal footing with the elite programs. Some of these cash cow departments could end up charging less but realize more net revenue than they do in the current environment (Winston 1994). The elite programs, such as engineering and business, might be able to charge more, but they too would face limits in their ability to charge consumers to support their own salaries. Some large public institutions have already moved in this direction as a result of cost-centered tuition (see, e.g., Berg and Hoenack 1987) and efforts to respond to the rescission of state budgets. If such assignments are made through the administrative structure to deans and department chairs without an emphasis on the faculty's involvement, however, then the potential to reduce inequities could be subverted.

More important, attempts to change the financial incentive structure could encourage faculty to pursue meaningful improvements in productivity by developing educational practices that reduce students' costs (i.e., improving retention and other educational outcomes). Present incentives clearly are for faculty to treat new technologies, such as computers and multimedia stations, as enhancements. If the financial incentive structure were adjusted, however, then faculty could realize some personal economic and professional gains for using technology to improve educational productivity. Further, faculty would have an economic incentive to be more nurturing toward students, encouraging their academic and social integration into the college environment, moving toward cultures that value the whole student (see, e.g., Rice and Austin 1988).

Incremental changes

Three areas of concern about the financial strategies used in colleges and universities emerge as crucial from the review of research on changes in financial strategy: administrative productivity, academic productivity, and pricing (tuition and student aid). The reconstructed financial framework proposes using action inquiry as a means of linking incremental policy decisions with systemic planning and budgeting. It is possible to achieve these links by changing the managerial processes used, either through the internal incentive structure or through a combined approach.

Before discussing the three priority areas, however, it is important to revisit the concept of empowerment coupled with responsibility. In higher education, faculty are empowered to make certain educational decisions, but they bear no financial responsibility for their actions. Similarly, administrators in service units are also empowered to engage directly in improving service delivery, but they are not always responsible for the financial consequences of their actions. This issue is fundamentally different from empowerment in public schools (e.g., Hopfenberg, Levin, and Associates 1993), where states and districts have made many basic educational and financial decisions. Thus, any discussion of empowerment in higher education should recognize the ambiguous situation that currently exists in most colleges and universities.

Administrative productivity. At least two issues that merit consideration by colleges and universities are concerned with creating meaningful incentives for administrative staff to embrace the issue of productivity: financial responsibility and action inquiry.

First, the prospect of experimenting with the financial incentive structure within administrative units merits consideration. Specifically, administrators have incentives to increase their staff allocations, which are generally related to compensation. And staff have incentives to increase production costs. The possibility of treating administrative units as cost centers merits exploration. For example, it is possible that if a student service unit reduces the percentage of the budget it requires, then a portion of the "savings" could be allocated to the unit (or perhaps to the staff member) to be used for bonuses, travel, and so forth. Such changes could be implemented through adaptation of current management practices in many instances. Another possibility is that student service units and auxiliary services could be run as "profit centers," with some form of reward distributed when "profit" is generated. These examples illustrate the fact that financial incentives can be created within administrative units. Unfortunately, many public universities are run as extensions of state civil service systems, which provide certain limited protections to staff but also limit the staff's willingness to cooperate in strategies aimed at improving cost structures.

Second, action inquiry provides a potential means for discovering better ways of providing educational services, especially if it is more directly linked to the process of making financial decisions. During the past decade, administrative practice in a number of specialty areas within higher education administration has been substantially improved. Efforts to improve enrollment management (see, e.g., Hossler 1987; Hossler, Bean, and Associates 1990) are particularly noteworthy: New marketing strategies have improved enrollment and new retention strategies have improved retention on many campuses. These efforts essentially improve financial conditions and reduce costs, as colleges with declining enrollments are more likely to have increased expenditures per student (Getz and Siegfried 1991). The link between the actions taken to improve enrollment and the costs (or savings) that result from these actions is seldom explicitly made, however. Therefore, in enrollment management, as in other areas of administration, it is possible to construct measures of meaningful productivity, especially long-term measures, that could be used as a basis of action experiments to assess innovations. More generally, administrative staffs—and the various specialty fields within educational administration (e.g., student financial aid, student personnel administration, admissions)—can be conceived of as fields in which professional action inquiry is encouraged and rewarded.

Academic productivity. The use of new incentives and action inquiry also applies to the faculty domain and to the prospect of realizing meaningful improvements in academic productivity. Faculty currently have incentives to reduce their teaching hours and the size of their classes. It is easy and nat-

Student service units and auxiliary services could be run as "profit centers," with some form of reward distributed when "profit" is generated.

ural for faculty to argue that students get a better education when faculty have fewer students. These conditions could be changed, however.

First, if financial decisions were delegated, then faculty would have more reason to critically examine their assumptions about class size and to experiment meaningfully with alternative approaches to academic productivity. It is also possible to make managerial adaptations that create an incentive linking changes in production of credit hours or provide financial incentives to programs to improve their retention rates. Such prospects even merit consideration by faculty unions as a means of creating a financial reward for improvements in teaching that result in meaningful gains in productivity.

Second, and more important, the prospect of engaging faculty in new forms of experimentation aimed at meaningful improvements in educational outcomes and the financial conditions of their institutions is an exciting possibility. A recent experiment conducted by a faculty member at Yavapai College, for example, illustrates the potential for using action inquiry to promote meaningful gains in academic productivity. An instructor in biology used a multimedia station to develop a multimedia program for his entry-level biology course (Lovell and Rooth 1994). Two sections of the class were offered, using the same textbooks, lecture notes, and examinations. The primary difference between the two course was that one used a multimedia format to enhance the delivery. The students in the section that used the multimedia format scored significantly better on every test and had a significantly lower dropout rate (26 percent compared to 20 percent). Further, a regression analysis indicated that the method, and not students' backgrounds, influenced the differences in test scores. From this preliminary assessment of this action experiment, it appears that the use of a multimedia format for teaching could pay for itself in terms of gains in student outcomes (and revenues from higher enrollment) as well as potentially extend opportunities (although the experiment did not explicitly address the costs of using various media).

The potential for uses of action inquiry as a means of promoting meaningful gains in productivity—and of linking improvements in instructional methods to reductions in costs—extends well beyond issues related to the integration of technology. The need also exists for more action-oriented inquiry into how variations in class size and instructional methods influence learning outcomes and into ways of improving academic integration and student retention (Guskin 1994). Some research has established ways of looking at the links between certain types of actions and student outcomes (Pascarella and Terenzini 1991), but action inquiry aimed at improving these outcomes has been more limited. Now is an opportune time for colleges and universities to provide incentives for interested faculty to initiate such discipline-based inquiries, assuming that meaningful variations exist in methods and outcomes across cognate fields.

Pricing. A belief has emerged during the past decade that students, especially those in public colleges, are not price-sensitive. Yet evidence is growing that students do indeed respond to prices and to price subsidies. The concept of differentiated prices (St. John and Starkey *In press*) provides a basis for thinking more systematically and critically about this link. Indeed, new approaches to evaluating the effects of student aid (St. John and Somers *In press;* Somers and St. John *In press*) and to assessing the likely effects of pricing alternatives (St. John 1993b, 1994a; Trammell 1994) have been developed, which can be used to guide action-oriented inquiries in this area.

The most crucial issue related to the effects of pricing that policy makers at all levels of the educational enterprise must understand is that pricing is a recursive process: Each new set of actions (that is, changes in tuition and aid strategies) influences not only the intended outcomes (such as first-time enrollment and retention), but also the ways students respond to prices and price subsidies (the linking mechanism between prices and enrollment). Given this evolving context, action inquiry—treating each new set of tuition and aid policies as "action experiments" that require testing in practice—is the most appropriate way to approach policy decisions about tuition and student aid. It is not possible to construct universal indicators (price-response measures) that inform us how students respond to tuition or student aid in every instance. Rather, these measures need to be carefully constructed from relevant research.

A systematic approach to restructuring
Based on these considerations, it is possible to suggest a preliminary design for a systematic approach to restructuring.

Colleges and universities are now confronted by the need to think more systematically about the issues of higher education's affordability and academic productivity. The position taken here is that efforts to improve productivity need to emphasize a gain in meaningful productivity—that is, gains in educational outcomes that reduce college costs—and that efforts to improve higher education's affordability need to focus on the effects of tuition charges and student aid. These dual issues—productivity and affordability—can be the basis for a systematic restructuring that empowers faculty to engage in action inquiry aimed at improving educational outcomes. Such a process, outlined in preliminary fashion in the following paragraphs, would be most directly applicable to liberal arts colleges and community colleges, because their primary mission is teaching undergraduates. In such colleges, the links between productivity and affordability are explicit.

First, a systematic approach to restructuring would need to be compatible with, and indeed integrated into, the planning and governing processes used in the institution. Unlike elementary and secondary schools that have recently begun to engage in restructuring (see, e.g., Hopfenberg, Levin, and Associates 1993), colleges and universities already have highly evolved processes for governance and planning. Therefore, consideration of financial strategy should first be integrated into these processes. Three types of actions would be needed to begin this process: assessing current academic and financial strategies to build an understanding of current problems and concerns; developing a vision (or set of goals) that explicitly addresses productivity and affordability; and, based on these insights, identifying "challenge areas" that merit action inquiry. Coordinating, or steering, the action inquiry should be integrated into the process of governance.

Second, action inquiry by teams of faculty and administrators, addressing challenges they have identified, can then become the basis for incremental and dynamic organizational learning. College teams could be organized to address challenge areas. Challenges that cut across administrative and academic departments would need diverse representation, while challenges that face departments or programs could be addressed by those academic units. As part of the process, for example, a program faculty might identify such challenges as improving learning outcomes as a means of improving students' persistence, reducing unit costs, and improving affordability. In the process of addressing a challenge, the faculty might negotiate with the administration to give them financial incentives for increasing their loads. They might also conceive of using a multimedia format to supplement instruction or using critical thinking to improve learning outcomes. Once faculty members understand the challenge, then they can design action experiments to test whether the proposed practices had the intended effects. Through such an organizational learning process, the incentive structure could be changed, turning faculty discontent into a positive force for dealing with underlying problems.

As another example, a college team might be formed with representation from across academic and administrative units to address a challenge to reduce the number of upper-division students transferring to other colleges. Such a team could examine a wide range of possible reasons for the problem: prices, availability of upper-division courses, and so forth. They could use action inquiry to more fully explore why the challenge exists and what types of actions might improve retention. Action experiments could be designed to test whether the solutions they picked actually improved the intended outcomes. By using experiments, the team could learn which types of strategies actually helped them to deal constructively with the challenge. To the extent that a college improved enrollment through deliberate experiment, it could reduce production costs and improve affordability.

Both these examples illustrate how teams of administrators and faculty within a college can use action inquiry to address challenges they identify. While many other managerial processes, such as enrollment management and total quality management, similarly emphasize problem solving, these methods usually do not explicitly link systemic and incremental changes with an explicit consideration of both financial and academic strategies. Through this type of process, colleges might also be able to make meaningful changes in their internal incentive structures so that faculty and administrators can receive financial rewards—as well as intrinsic satisfaction—for their efforts to improve productivity and affordability.

Finally, the process of restructuring needs to be field tested over several years. In the first year, colleges would assess their current financial and academic strategies, develop a vision that incorporates consideration of financial (productivity and affordability) and academic goals, identify challenge areas, and form action teams to explore the challenge areas and identify "action experiments" that could be pilot tested. In the second year, the action teams would conduct and assess their action experiments, communicating their progress and results to the college communities as appropriate, and continue to assess issues related to their challenge area and develop new experiments. In the third year, colleges would begin to make systemic changes as appropriate, based on the understandings they developed from the action experiments. It would also be important, however, to continue assessing, envisioning, and identifying systemwide challenges and have teams of faculty and administrators continue to use action inquiry to address challenge areas. In other words, restructuring could become a dynamic, ongoing process that involves both action inquiry and systemic reforms.

The Crisis of College Costs in Perspective

The current controversy over college costs can be viewed in at least two ways. One possible lens is to assume that college revenues are determined by economic conditions (see, e.g., Froomkin 1990; Hauptman 1992). If we hold this belief, assuming that external economic forces determine our future, then we can conclude we will be better off waiting until the economy improves. Taking this posture, however, entails the growing risk of having cost controls externally imposed.

In 1994–95, most states received increased tax revenues (Church 1994), and the percentage increase in state student grants was slightly larger than in tuition (National Association 1994). While these facts could be viewed as support of the wait-and-see philosophy, it appears that, in response to the increase in revenue, states are concerned about reducing tax rates (Church 1994) rather than reinvesting in higher education. Therefore, an alternative path is needed, one that involves taking more responsibility for the financial issues we face and communicates a more positive image of colleges and universities as productive organizations.

The alternative is to dig beneath the surface of this emerging crisis, examine the forces that have contributed to our present predicament, and experiment with new strategies that could lead to meaningful improvements. If one takes this approach, then economic conditions are recognized as being important, but it is also possible to identify action strategies that institutions, states, and the federal government can take.

If members of the academic community take this alternative view, then it is possible to envision opportunities for meaningful change. In particular, it is possible to see how the methods of inquiry that are so vital to academic communities can be used to make colleges and universities better places to work and learn. On the one hand, we can wait and see what external forces impose on us. On the other, we can begin to take some personal and professional responsibility for improving our learning communities by helping them to adapt to a rapidly changing world.

REFERENCES

The Educational Resources Information Center (ERIC) Clearinghouse on Higher Education abstracts and indexes the current literature on higher education for inclusion in ERIC's data base and announcement in ERIC's monthly bibliographic journal, *Resources in Education* (RIE). Most of these publications are available through the ERIC Document Reproduction Service (EDRS). For publications cited in this bibliography that are available from EDRS, ordering number and price code are included. Readers who wish to order a publication should write to the ERIC Document Reproduction Service, 7420 Fullerton Rd., Suite 110, Springfield, VA 22153-2852. (Phone orders with VISA or MasterCard are taken at 800-443-ERIC or 703-440-1400.) When ordering, please specify the document (ED) number. Documents are available as noted in microfiche (MF) and paper copy (PC). If you have the price code ready when you call EDRS, an exact price can be quoted. The last page of the latest issue of *Resources in Education* also has the current cost, listed by code.

Advanced Technology, Inc., and Westat Research, Inc. 1983. "Preliminary Report on Assessment of 1982–83 Pell Grant Program." Reston, Va.: Advanced Technology, Inc.

————. 1987. Quality Control Study, Stage 2. *Final Report: Executive Summary.* Reston, Va.: Advanced Technology, Inc.

Alexander, Kern. Spring 1976. "The Value of an Education." *Journal of Education Finance* 1: 429–67.

Alsalam, Nabeel, Gayle E. Fischer, Lawrence T. Ogle, Gayle Thompson Rogers, and Thomas M. Smith. 1993. *The Condition of Education 1993.* Washington, D.C.; National Center for Education Statistics. ED 357 513. 511 pp. MF–02; PC–21.

American Association of University Professors, American Council on Education, and Association of Governing Boards. 1966. "Statement on Governance of Colleges and Universities." *Academe* 52(4): 375–79.

American Council on Education. 27 December 1991. "State Fiscal Problems Hit Higher Education Enrollment, ACE Survey Shows." Press release. Washington, D.C.: Author.

Anderson, Harriet. 18 May 1987. "Fuming over College Costs: Increasingly Middle-Class Families Face Sacrifice, Debt, and Hard Choices." *Newsweek:* 66–71.

Anderson, Richard E. 1987. "Tuition Purchase Plans: Why They're Needed and What's at Stake." *Change* 19(2): 36–41.

Andrieu, Sandra C., and Edward P. St. John. 1993. "The Influence of Prices on Graduate Student Persistence." *Research in Higher Education* 34(4): 399–426.

Argyris, Chris, Robert Putnam, and Diana McLain Smith. 1985. *Action Science.* San Francisco: Jossey-Bass.

Associated Press. 27 December 1993. "Big Decline in Enrollment at Colleges." *San Francisco Chronicle.*

Association of Governing Boards. 1986. "The Tuition Booklet." Washington, D.C.: Author. ED 276 360. 7 pp. MF–01; PC–01.

Astin, Alexander W. 1975. *Preventing Students from Dropping Out.* San Francisco: Jossey-Bass.

Atwell, Robert H., and Arthur M. Hauptman. 1986. "The Politics of Tuition." *Educational Record* 67(2–3): 5–6.

Baird, Leonard L. 1991. "Publication Productivity in Doctoral Research Departments: Interdisciplinary and Intradisciplinary Factors." *Research in Higher Education* 32(3): 303–18.

Balderston, Fredric C. 1974. *Managing Today's University.* San Francisco: Jossey-Bass.

Bassett, W. Bruce. 1983. "Cost Control in Higher Education." In *The Crisis in Higher Education,* edited by J. Froomkin. New York: Academy of Political Science.

Bean, John P. 1980. "Dropouts and Turnover: The Synthesis of a Causal Model of Student Attrition." *Research in Higher Education* 12: 155–87.

———. 1982. "Conceptual Models of Student Attrition: How Theory Can Help the Institutional Researcher." In *Studying Student Attrition,* edited by E. Pascarella. New Directions for Institutional Research No. 36. San Francisco: Jossey-Bass.

———. 1985. "Interaction Effects Based on Class Level in an Explanatory Model of College Student Dropout Syndrome." *American Education Research Journal* 22: 35–64.

Bean, John P., and B. Metzner. 1985. "A Conceptual Model of Nontraditional Student Attrition." *Review of Educational Research* 55: 485–540.

Becker, Gary S. 1964. *Human Capital: A Theoretical and Empirical Analysis with Special Reference to Education.* New York: National Bureau of Economic Research.

Bennett, William J. 26 November 1986. "Text of Secretary Bennett's Speech on College Costs and U.S. Student Aid." *Chronicle of Higher Education:* 20.

———. 18 February 1987. "Our Greedy Colleges." *New York Times.*

Berg, David J., and Stephen A. Hoenack. 1987. "The Concept of Cost-Related Tuition and Its Implications at the University of Minnesota." *Journal of Higher Education* 58: 276–395.

Blackburn, Robert T., Jeffery P. Bieber, Janet H. Lawrence, and Lois Trautvelter. 1991. "Faculty at Work: Focus on Research, Scholarship, and Service." *Research in Higher Education* 32(4): 385–413.

Bluestone, Barry. 1993. "UMass/Boston: An Economic Impact Analysis." Boston: University of Massachusetts at Boston.

Bowen, Howard R. 1980. *The Cost of Higher Education.* San Francisco: Jossey-Bass.

Braybrook, D., and Charles E. Lindblom. 1963. *A Strategy of Decision:*

Policy Evaluation as a Social Process. New York: Free Press.

Brimelow, Peter. 30 November 1987. "The Untouchables." *Forbes:* 141–50.

Brinkman, Paul T. May/June 1981. "Factors Affecting Instructional Costs at Major Research Universities." *Journal of Higher Education* 52: 265–79.

Brinkman, Paul T., and Dennis P. Jones. 1987. "Comments." In *Estimating the Cost of a Bachelor's Degree: An Institutional Cost Analysis,* by Duc-Le To. Washington, D.C.: U.S. Dept. of Education, Office of Educational Research and Improvement. ED 283 499. 98 pp. MF–01; PC–04.

Brinkman, Paul T., and Deborah J. Teeters. 1987. "Methods of Selecting Comparison Groups." In *Conducting Institutional Comparisons,* edited by Paul T. Brinkman. New Directions in Higher Education No. 53. San Francisco: Jossey-Bass.

Brown, David G. 1988. "The University of North Carolina–Asheville." In *Successful Strategic Planning: Case Studies,* edited by Douglas W. Steeples. New Directions for Higher Education No. 64. San Francisco: Jossey-Bass.

Brunner, Ilse, and Wendy S. Hopfenberg. *In press.* "Growth and Learning in Accelerated Schools: Big Wheels and Little Wheels Interacting." In *Accelerated Schools in Action: Lessons from Research and Practice,* edited by Christine Finnan, Edward P. St. John, Simeon Slovacek, and Jane McCarthy. Newberry Park, Calif.: Corwin Press.

Bureau of the Census. 1983. "Lifetime Earnings Estimates for Men and Women in the United States: 1979." *Current Population Reports: Consumer Income.* Series P-60, No. 139. Washington, D.C.: U.S. Government Printing Office.

————. 1984. "What's It Worth? Educational Background and Economic Status: Spring 1984." *Current Population Reports: Household Economic Status.* Series P-70, No. 11. Washington, D.C.: U.S. Government Printing Office.

Cabrera, Alberto F., M.B. Castaneda, A. Nora, and D. Hengstler. 1992. "The Convergence between Two Theories of College Persistence." *Journal of Higher Education* 63(2): 143–64.

Cabrera, Alberto F., Jacob O. Stampen, and W. Lee Hansen. 1990. "Exploring the Effects of Ability to Pay in Persistence in College." *Review of Higher Education* 23(3): 303–36.

Califano, Joseph A. 18 August 1994. "What We Need Is a Clean and Lean Bill: Get the Junk Out." *Washington Post.*

Cameron, Kim S. 1984. "Organizational Adaptation and Higher Education." *Journal of Higher Education* 55(2): 122–44.

Carlson, Daryl E. 1975. "Examining Efficient Joint Production Processes." In *Measuring and Increasing Academic Productivity,* edited by R.A. Wallhaus. New Directions for Institutional Research

No. 5. San Francisco: Jossey-Bass.

———. 1977. *A Review of Production Function Estimation for Higher Education Institutions: The Development of Colleges and Universities.* Prepared for the U.S. Office of Education, Office of Planning, Budgeting, and Evaluation. Cambridge, Mass.: Harvard Univ., Graduate School of Education.

Chaffee, Ellen E. 1984. "Successful Strategic Management in Small Private Colleges." *Journal of Higher Education* 55(2): 212–41.

———. 1985. "The Concept of Strategy." In *Higher Education: Handbook of Theory and Research,* edited by J.C. Smart. Vol. 1. New York: Agathon Press.

———. 1989. "Strategy and Effectiveness in Higher Education." In *Higher Education: Handbook of Theory and Research,* edited by J.C. Smart. Vol. 5. New York: Agathon Press.

Chaffee, Ellen E., and Lawrence A. Sherr. 1992. *Quality: Transforming Postsecondary Education.* ASHE-ERIC Higher Education Report No. 3. Washington, D.C.: George Washington Univ., School of Education and Human Development. ED 351 922. 145 pp. MF–01; PC–06.

Chaikind, Stephen. ca. 1987. *College Enrollment Patterns by Black and White Students.* Prepared for the U.S. Dept. of Education, Planning and Evaluation Service. Washington, D.C.: DRC.

Cheit, Earl F. 1971. *The New Depression in Higher Education.* New York: McGraw-Hill.

———. 1973. *The New Depression in Higher Education—Two Years Later.* New York: McGraw-Hill.

Church, George J. 19 September 1994. "A Fever for Tax Cuts." *Time:* 43.

College Board. 1992. "Trends in Student Aid: 1982–1992." New York: Author. ED 353 867. 17 pp. MF–01; PC–01.

Congressional Budget Office. 1991. *Student Aid and the Cost of Postsecondary Education.* Washington, D.C.: Author. ED 329 158. 126 pp. MF–01; PC–06.

Council for Advancement and Support of Education. 1987. "Tuition: The Story and How to Tell It." Presented at a CASE senior seminar, Brown Univ., October 11–14.

Creech, Sandra K., Stan Carpenter, and Eddie Joe Davis. 1994. "The Direct Economic Impact of Texas's Appropriations to Higher Education." *Review of Higher Education* 17(2): 125–42.

Curry, Dennis J. 1988. *Tuition and Student Aid Policies: What Role for SHEEOs?* Denver: State Higher Education Executive Officers.

Cyert, Richard M. 1988. "Carnegie Mellon University." In *Successful Strategic Planning: Case Studies,* edited by Douglas W. Steeples. New Directions in Higher Education No. 64. San Francisco: Jossey-Bass.

Davis, Diane E., and Helen S. Astin. 1987. "Reputational Standing in Academe." *Journal of Higher Education* 58(3): 261–75.

Davis, Jerry S., Deborah Nastelli, and Kenneth E. Redd. 1993. *The National Association of State Scholarship and Grant Programs 24th Annual Survey Report: 1992–93 Academic Year.* Harrisburg: Pennsylvania Higher Education Assistance Agency.

Davis, Robert H., Rich Strand, Lawrence T. Alexander, and M. Norril Hussain. 1982. "The Impact of Organizational and Innovator Variables in Instructional Innovation in Higher Education." *Journal of Higher Education* 53(5): 568–86.

Dickmeyer, Nathan. 8 April 1983. "The Impact of Federal Student Financial Assistance on Tuition, Institutional Student Aid, and Alumni Giving." Prepared for the National Commission on Student Financial Assistance.

Dresch, Stephen P. 1975. "A Critique of Planning Models for Postsecondary Education: Current Feasibility, Potential Relevance, and a Prospectus for Future Research." *Journal of Higher Education* 46(3): 246–86.

Eiser, Lawrence, ed. 1988. *A Call for Clarity: Income, Loans, Cost.* Washington, D.C.: American Association of State Colleges and Universities. ED 293 397. 55 pp. MF–01; PC not available EDRS.

Etzioni, Amitai. 1964. *Modern Organizations.* Englewood Cliffs, N.J.: Prentice-Hall.

Evangelauf, Jean. 2 March 1988a. "Costs of Attending College Appear Likely to Rise Faster than Inflation for the Eighth Year in a Row." *Chronicle of Higher Education:* A29–A30.

———. 2 March 1988b. "President Says 100 Private Colleges Follow Crowd: The Higher Their Prices, the More Students Apply." *Chronicle of Higher Education:* A29–A30.

Feldman, Kenneth A. 1987. "Research Productivity and Scholarly Accomplishment of College Teachers as Related to Their Instructional Effectiveness: A Review and Synthesis." *Research in Higher Education* 26(3): 227–98.

Finn, Chester E. July/August 1988a. "Judgment Time for Higher Education: In the Court of Public Opinion." *Change:* 35–38.

———. 1988b. "Prepared Statement and Attachments." Hearing 15 September 1987 before the Subcommittee on Postsecondary Education, Committee on Education and Labor, House of Representatives, 100th Congress, 1st Session, No. 100-47. Washington, D.C.: U.S. Government Printing Office.

Fischer, Fredrick G. 1990. "State Financing of Higher Education: A New Look at an Old Problem." *Change* 22(1): 42–56.

Foote, Edward J. 1988. "The University of Miami." In *Successful Strategic Planning: Case Studies,* edited by Douglas W. Steeples. New Directions in Higher Education No. 64. San Francisco: Jossey-Bass.

Frances, Carol. 1985. "Why Tuition Keeps Going Up." *AGB Reports* 27(2): 24–31.

Freedberg, Louis. 27 December 1993. "Enrollment Dips 9 Percent at Community Colleges." *San Francisco Chronicle.*

Freeman, Richard B. 1976. *The Overeducated American.* New York: Academic Press.

Friedman, Milton. 1962. *Capitalism and Freedom.* Chicago: Univ. of Chicago Press.

Froomkin, Joseph. 1990. "Impact of Changing Levels of Financial Resources on the Structures of Colleges and Universities." In *The Economics of American Universities,* edited by Stephen A. Hoenack and Eileen L. Collins. Albany: State Univ. of New York Press.

Garvin, David A. 1980. *The Economics of University Behavior.* New York: Academic Press.

Gerald, Debra E., and William J. Hussar. 1990. *Projections of Educational Statistics to 2001.* Washington, D.C.: National Center for Education Statistics. ED 327 581. 201 pp. MF–01; PC–09.

Getz, Malcolm, and John J. Siegfried. 1991. "Cost and Productivity in American Colleges and Universities." In *Economic Challenges in Higher Education,* edited by Charles T. Clofelter et al. Chicago: Univ. of Chicago Press.

Girling, Robert H., George Goldman, and Sherry Keith. 1993. *Economic Impact of the California State University on the California Economy: 1993–2002.* Sonoma, Calif.: Sonoma State Univ.

Gladieux, Lawrence E., and Thomas R. Wolanin. 1976. *Congress and the Colleges.* Lexington, Mass.: Heath.

Golden, John, and Fred V. Carstensen. 1992. "Academic Research Productivity, Department Size, and Organization: Further Results, Comments." *Economics of Education Review* 11(2): 153–60.

Green, Kenneth C. 15 September 1987. "College Costs and Student Aid." Statement prepared for public hearings on college costs held by the Subcommittee on Postsecondary Education, U.S. House of Representatives, Washington, D.C. ED 286 424. 10 pp. MF–01; PC–01.

Griswold, Carolyn P., and Ginger M. Marine. *In press.* "Political Influences on State Tuition-Aid Policy: Higher Tuition/Higher Aid and the Real World." *Research in Higher Education.*

Grubb, W. Norton. 1993. "The Long-Term Effects of Proprietary Schools on Wages and Earnings: Implications for Federal Policy." *Educational Evaluation and Policy Analysis* 15(1): 17–33.

———. 1994. "The Long-Term Effects of Proprietary Schools: Corrections." *Educational Evaluation and Policy Analysis* 16(3): 351–56.

Gumport, Patricia. 1993. "The Contested Terrain of Academic Program Reduction." *Journal of Higher Education* 64(3): 283–311.

Guskin, Alan E. 1994. "Reducing Student Costs and Enhancing Student Learning. Part II: Restructuring the Role of Faculty." *Change* 26(5): 16–33.

Habermas, Jurgen. 1984. *The Theory of Communicative Action.* Vol.

1, *Reason and the Rationalization of Society.* Translated by T. McCarthy. Boston: Beacon Press.

———. 1987. *The Theory of Communicative Action.* Vol. 2, *Lifeworld and System: A Critique of Functionalist Reason.* Translated by T. McCarthy. Boston: Beacon Press.

———. 1991. *Moral Consciousness and Communicative Action.* Translated by C. Lenhardt and S.W. Nicholsen. Cambridge, Mass.: MIT Press.

———. 1992. *The New Conservatism: Cultural Criticism and the Historians' Debate.* Translated by S.B. Nicholsen. Cambridge, Mass.: MIT Press.

Halstead, D. Kent. 1974. *Statewide Planning in Higher Education.* Washington, D.C.: U.S. Government Printing Office. ED 096 914. 860 pp. MF–05; PC–35.

Hansen, W. Lee. 1983. "Impact of Student Financial Aid on Access." In *The Crisis in Higher Education,* edited by J. Froomkin. New York: Academy of Political Science.

Hauptman, Arthur M. 1990a. *The College Tuition Spiral.* New York: Macmillan.

———. 1990b. *The Tuition Dilemma: Assessing New Ways to Pay for College.* Washington, D.C.: Brookings Institution.

———. 1991. *New Ways of Paying for College.* New York: Macmillan.

———. 1992. *The Economic Prospects for American Higher Education.* Washington, D.C.: Association of Governing Boards/American Council on Education. ED 350 903. 36 pp. MF–01; PC–02.

———. 1993. "Alternatives for Funding Postsecondary Education: Pricing Structures and Financial Aid." In *Financing Higher Education in the 21st Century: A Summary of Seminars and a National Symposium,* edited by J.P. Merisotis. Washington, D.C.: National Commission on Responsibilities for Financing Postsecondary Education.

Hauptman, Arthur M., and Terry Hartle. 23 February 1987. "Tuition Increases since 1970: A Perspective." *Higher Education and National Affairs.* Newsletter. Washington, D.C.: American Council on Education.

Hauptman, Arthur M., and Dave Roose. 1993. "Trends in Paying for Higher Education, 1950–1990." In *Background Papers and Reports,* edited by J.P. Merisotis. Washington, D.C.: National Commission on Responsibilities for Financing Postsecondary Education.

Haveman, Robert. 1988. *Starting Even: An Equal Opportunity Program to Combat the Nation's New Poverty.* New York: Simon & Schuster.

Hearn, James C. 1987. "Strategy and Resources: Economic Issues in State Planning and Management in Higher Education." In *Higher Education: Handbook of Theory and Research,* edited by J.C. Smart. Vol. 4. New York: Agathon Press.

———. 1993. "The Paradox of Growth in Federal Aid for College Students: 1965–1990. In *Higher Education: Handbook of Theory and Research,* edited by J.C. Smart. Vol. 9. New York: Agathon Press.

Hearn, James C., and Melissa S. Anderson. 1989. "Integrating Post-secondary Education Financing Policies: The Minnesota Model." In *Studying the Impact of Student Aid on Institutions,* edited by R.H. Fenske. New Directions in Institutional Research No. 62. San Francisco: Jossey-Bass.

Hearn, James C., and Carolyn P. Griswold. 1994. "State-Level Innovation in U.S. Postsecondary Education." *Educational Evaluation and Policy Analysis* 16(2): 161–90.

Hearn, James C., and David Longanecker. 1985. "Enrollment Effects of Alternative Postsecondary Pricing Policies." *Journal of Higher Education* 56(5): 485–508.

Hines, Edward R. 1988. *Higher Education and State Governments: Renewed Partnership, Cooperation, or Competition?* ASHE-ERIC Higher Education Report No. 5. Washington, D.C.: Association for the Study of Higher Education. ED 306 840. 177 pp. MF–01; PC–08.

———. 1993. *State Higher Education Appropriations, 1992–93.* Denver: State Higher Education Executive Officers. ED 365 262. 50 pp. MF–01; PC–02.

Hoenack, Stephen A. 1983. *Economic Behavior within Organizations.* Cambridge, Eng.: Cambridge Univ. Press.

Hopfenberg, Wendy S., Henry M. Levin, and Associates. 1993. *Accelerated Schools Resource Guide.* San Francisco: Jossey-Bass.

Hossler, Don. 1984. *Enrollment Management: An Integrated Approach.* New York: College Entrance Examination Board.

———. 1987. *Creating Effective Enrollment Management Systems.* New York: College Entrance Examination Board.

Hossler, Don, John P. Bean, and Associates. 1990. *The Strategic Management of College Enrollment.* San Francisco: Jossey-Bass.

Institute for Research on Higher Education, University of Pennsylvania. 1994. "The Landscape. Where the Jobs Are: College Graduates and Job Prospects." *Change* 26(1): 33–36.

Iosue, Robert J. June 1988. "Controlling Costs for a Lean Administration." *College Services Administration:* 20–51.

Jackson, Gregory A. 1978. "Financial Aid and Student Enrollment." *Journal of Higher Education* 49(6): 548–74.

———. 1988. "Did College Choice Change during the 1970s?" *Economics of Education Review* 7(1): 15–27.

Jackson, Gregory A., and George B. Weathersby. 1975. "Individual Demand for Higher Education." *Journal of Higher Education* 46(6): 623–52.

Jackson-Beeck, Marilyn, Scott Leitz, J. Vos, and John Yunker. 1994. *Higher Education Tuition and State Grants.* Minneapolis: Minnesota Office of Legislative Auditor, Program Evaluation Div.

Jacobi, Maryann, Alexander Astin, and Frank Ayala, Jr. 1987. *College Student Outcomes Assessment: A Talent Development Perspective.* ASHE-ERIC Higher Education Report No. 7. Washington, D.C.: Association for the Study of Higher Education. ED 296 693. 141 pp. MF–01; PC–06.

Jacobs, Fredric, and Tyler Tingley. 1977. *The Evolution of Eligibility Criteria for Title III of the Higher Education Act of 1965. The Development of Colleges and Universities.* Cambridge, Mass.: Harvard Univ., Graduate School of Education.

Jacobson, Robert L. 15 April 1992. "Colleges Face New Pressure to Increase Faculty Productivity." *Chronicle of Higher Education:* A1+.

Kaltenbaugh, Louise P. 1993. "The Influence of Prices and Price Subsidies on Within-Year Persistence by African-Americans." Doctoral dissertation, Univ. of New Orleans.

Keller, George A. 1983. *Academic Strategy.* Baltimore: Johns Hopkins Univ. Press.

King, S., and Lee M. Wolfle. 1987. "A Latent-Variable Causal Model of Faculty Reputational Ratings." *Research in Higher Education* 27(2): 99–106.

Kirshstein, Rita J., Daniel J. Sherman, Valentina K. Tikoff, Charles Masten, and James Fairweather. 1990. *The Escalating Costs of Higher Education.* Prepared for the U.S. Dept. of Education, Office of Planning, Budget, and Evaluation. Washington, D.C.: Pelavin Associates. ED 328 114. 161 pp. MF–01; PC–07.

Kirshstein, Rita, Valentina K. Tikoff, Charles Masten, and Edward P. St. John. 1990. *Trends in Institutional Costs.* Prepared for the U.S. Dept. of Education, Office of Planning, Budget, and Evaluation. Washington, D.C.: Pelavin Associates. ED 328 115. 125 pp. MF–01; PC–05.

Knutsen, Kirk L. 1993. *Beyond Business as Usual: A Framework and Options for Improving Quality and Containing Costs in California Higher Education.* CRB-OP-93-001. Sacramento: Calif. State Library, Calif. Research Bureau.

Konrad, Alison M., and Jeffrey Pfeffer. 1990. "Do You Get What You Deserve? Factors Affecting the Relationship between Productivity and Pay." *Administrative Science Quarterly* 35(2): 258–85.

Kotler, Phillip, and Patrick E. Murphy. 1981. "Strategic Planning for Higher Education." *Journal of Higher Education* 52: 470–89.

Kramer, Martin. 1993a. "Changing Roles in Higher Education Finance." In *Background Papers and Reports,* edited by J.P. Merisotis. Washington, D.C.: National Commission on Responsibilities for Financing Postsecondary Education.

———. 1993b. "Toward a More Stable Allocation of Financing Roles." In *Financing Higher Education in the 21st Century,* edited by J.P. Merisotis. Washington, D.C.: National Commission on Responsibilities for Financing Postsecondary Education.

———. 1994. "Earning and Learning: Are Students Working Too Much?" *Change* 26(1): 6–7.

Lawrence, Janet H., and Robert T. Blackburn. 1988. "Age as a Predictor of Faculty Productivity: Three Conceptual Approaches." *Journal of Higher Education* 59(1): 22–38.

Layzell, Daniel T., and Jan W. Lyddon. 1990. *Budgeting for Higher Education at the State Level.* ASHE-ERIC Higher Education Report No. 4. Washington, D.C.: George Washington Univ., School of Education and Human Development. ED 327 130. 134 pp. MF–01; PC–06.

Leatherman, Courtney. 9 February 1994. "Accreditors Fight Back: Hoping to Fend Off Government, They Ponder Changes in the Way They Assess Colleges." *Chronicle of Higher Education:* A21–22.

Leslie, Larry L. 1990. "Rates of Return as Informer of Public Policy: With Special Consideration to the World Bank and Third World Countries." *Higher Education* 20: 271–86.

Leslie, Larry L., and Paul T. Brinkman. 1986. "Rates of Return to Higher Education: An Intensive Examination." In *Higher Education: Handbook of Theory and Research,* edited by J.C. Smart. New York: Agathon Press.

———. 1987. "Student Price Response in Higher Education: The Student Demand Studies." *Journal of Higher Education* 58(2): 181–204.

———. 1988. *The Economic Value of Higher Education.* San Francisco: Jossey-Bass.

Levin, Henry M. 1983. *Cost Effectiveness: A Primer. New Perspectives in Evaluation.* Vol. 4. Beverly Hills, Calif.: Sage.

———. 1986. *Educational Reform for Disadvantaged Students: An Emerging Crisis.* West Haven, Conn.: NEA Professional Library.

———. 1987. "Accelerated Schools for Disadvantaged Students." *Educational Leadership* 44(6): 47–60.

———. 1991. "Raising Productivity in Higher Education." *Journal of Higher Education* 62(3): 241–62.

Lewis, Gwendolyn L. 1989. "Trends in Student Aid: 1963–64 to 1988–89." *Research in Higher Education* 30: 547–62.

Lindblom, Charles E. 1977. *Politics and Markets: The World's Political and Economic Systems.* New York: Basic Books.

Lindblom, Charles E., and David K. Cohen. 1979. *Usable Knowledge: Social Science and Social Problem Solving.* New Haven, Conn.: Yale Univ. Press.

Lisensky, Robert P. 1988. "Integrating Control Systems." In *Successful Strategic Planning: Case Studies,* edited by Douglas W. Steeples. New Directions in Higher Education No. 64. San Francisco: Jossey-Bass.

Lopez, M. 7 April 1993. "High Tuition, High Aid Won't Work." *Chron-*

icle of Higher Education: B1–B2.

Lovell, Terry D., and Stewart Rooth. 1994. "Assessment Report on Institutional Research: BSA 131 Multimedia vs. Traditional Lecture." Prescott, Ariz.: Yavapai Community College.

McCarthy, P., S. Meier, and R. Rindera. 1985. "Self-Efficacy and Writing: A Different View of Self-Evaluation." *College Compensation and Communication* 36(4): 465–71.

McLaughlin, Gerald W., James R. Montgomery, Alvin W. Smith, Beatrice T. Mahan, and Lawrence T. Broomall. 1980. "Size and Efficiency." *Research in Higher Education* 12(1): 53–66.

McPherson, Michael S. 1978. "The Demand for Higher Education." In *Public Policy and Private Higher Education,* edited by David W. Breneman and Chester E. Finn. Washington, D.C.: Brookings Institution.

McPherson, Michael S., and Morton Owen Schapiro. 1991. *Keeping College Affordable: Government and Educational Opportunity.* Washington, D.C.: Brookings Institution.

Manski, Charles F., and David A. Wise. 1983. *College Choice in America.* Cambridge, Mass.: Harvard Univ. Press.

Martin, David. May 1988. "Understanding the Costs of College." *Phi Delta Kappan:* 673–76.

Massy, William F., and Andrea Wilger. Winter 1992. "Productivity in Postsecondary Education: A New Approach." *Education Evaluation and Policy Analysis:* 361–76.

Massy, William F., and Robert Zemsky. 1992. "Faculty Discretionary Time: Departments and the Academic Ratchet." Discussion Paper No. 4. Stanford, Calif.: Stanford Institute of Higher Education Research.

Matkin, Gary W. 17 November 1993. "Colleges as Promoters of Economic Development." *Chronicle of Higher Education:* B1–B2.

Merisotis, Jamie P., ed. 1993. *Financing Higher Education in the 21st Century: A Summary of Seminars and a National Symposium.* Washington, D.C.: National Commission on Responsibilities for Financing Postsecondary Education.

Mingle, James R. 1987. *Focus on Minorities: Trends in Higher Education Participation and Success.* Denver: Education Commission of the States/State Higher Education Executive Officers. ED 287 404. 50 pp. MF–01; PC–02.

———. 1988a. "Effective Coordination of Higher Education: What Is It? Why Is It So Difficult?" *Issues in Higher Education* No. 23.

———. 1988b. *Survey of Tuition Policy, Costs, and Student Aid.* Denver: State Higher Education Executive Officers.

Minnesota Higher Education Coordinating Board. 18 August 1994. "The Design for Shared Responsibility." Staff Background Paper No. 3. Minneapolis: Author.

Mortensen, Thomas G. 1987. "Change in College Enrollment Mo-

tivation for White and Black College Freshmen, 1978–1984." In
*Proceedings of the Fourth Annual NASSGP/NCHELP Conference
on Student Financial Aid Research,* June 3–5, 1987, St. Louis, Missouri. Vol. 1. Albany: New York State Higher Education Services
Corp.

Muffo, John A., Susan V. Mead, and Alan E. Bayer. 1987. "Using Faculty
Publication Rates to Compare 'Peer' Institutions." *Research in
Higher Education* 27(2): 163–75.

National Association of College and University Business Officers.
1988. *Capital Formation Alternatives in Higher Education.*
Washington, D.C.: Author.

———. 1994. "State Spending on Student Aid up 12.6 Percent, Study
Finds." *NACUBO Business Office* 28(3): 13.

National Commission on the Financing of Postsecondary Education.
1973. *Financing Postsecondary Education in the United States.*
Washington, D.C.: U.S. Government Printing Office. ED 086 042.
472 pp. MF–01; PC–19.

National Commission on Responsibilities for Financing Postsecondary Education. 1993. *Making College Affordable Again. Final
Report.* Washington, D.C.: Author. ED 351 995. 103 pp. MF–01;
PC–05.

National Institute of Independent Colleges and Universities. 1987.
The Truth about Costs in the Independent Sector of Higher Education. Washington, D.C.: Author.

Norris, Donald M., and Nicholas C. Poulton. 1987. *A Guide for New
Planners.* Ann Arbor, Mich.: Society for College and University
Planners.

O'Keefe, Michael. November/December 1987. "Where Does the
Money Really Go?" *Change:* 12–34. ED 299 892. 71 pp. MF–01;
PC–03.

O'Neill, Dave, and Peter Sepielli. 1988. *Education in the United
States: 1940–1983.* Special Demographic Analysis CDS 85-1.
Washington, D.C.: U.S. Bureau of the Census.

Pascarella, Ernest T., John C. Smart, and M.A. Smylie. 1992. "College
Tuition Costs and Early Socioeconomic Achievement: Do You Get
What You Pay For?" *Higher Education* 24: 275–90.

Pascarella, Ernest T., John C. Smart, and Judith Stoecker. 1989. "College, Race, and the Early Status Attainment of Black Students." *Journal of Higher Education* 60(1): 82–107.

Pascarella, Ernest T., and Patrick T. Terenzini. 1979. "Interaction
Effects in Spady's and Tinto's Conceptual Models of College Dropout." *Sociology of Education* 52: 197–210.

———. 1980. "Predicting Voluntary Freshman Year Persistence/Withdrawal Behavior in a Residential University: A Path Analytic Validation of Tinto's Model." *Journal of Educational Psychology*
51(1): 60–75.

———. 1988. "Predicting Freshman Persistence and Voluntary Drop-out Decisions from a Theoretical Model." *Journal of Higher Education* 51(1): 60–75.

———. 1991. *How College Affects Students.* San Francisco: Jossey-Bass.

Paulos, John Allen. 7 August 1994. "Math for the Year 2×10^3: Resetting Our Goals." *Washington Post.*

Paulsen, Michael B. Summer 1989. "Estimating Instructional Cost Functions at Small Private Colleges." *Journal of Educational Finance* 15: 53–66.

———. 1990. *College Choice: Understanding Student Enrollment Behavior.* ASHE-ERIC Higher Education Report No. 6. Washington, D.C.: George Washington Univ., School of Education and Human Development. ED 333 855. 121 pp. MF–01; PC–05.

———. 1991. "College Tuition: Determinants 1960 to 1986." *Review of Higher Education* 14(3): 339–58.

———. 1994. "The Effects of Higher Education on Workforce Productivity in the Fifty States." Paper presented at an annual meeting of the American Educational Research Association, April, New Orleans, Louisiana.

Pelavin, Sol H., and Michael B. Kane. 1988. *Minority Participation in Higher Education.* Washington, D.C.: Pelavin Associates.

———. 1990. *Change the Odds: Factors Increasing Access to College.* New York: College Board.

Pellino, Glenn R., Robert T. Blackburn, and Alice L. Boberg. 1984. "The Dimensions of Academic Scholarship: Faculty and Administration Views." *Research in Higher Education* 20(1): 103–15.

Perrucci, Robert, Kathleen O'Flaherty, and Harvey Marshall. 1983. "Market Conditions, Productivity, and Promotion among University Faculty." *Research in Higher Education* 19(4): 431–49.

Peterson, Rose D. 1994. "The Proprietary School Dilemma: A Case Study." Predissertation research, Univ. of New Orleans.

Pfeffer, J., and W. Moore. 1980. "Power and Politics in University Budgeting: A Replication and Extension." *Administrative Science Quarterly* 25: 637–53.

Putka, Gary. 11 December 1987. "Tracking Tuition: Why College Fees Are Rising So Sharply." *Wall Street Journal.*

Rhoades, Gary. 1993. "Retrenchment Clauses in Faculty Union Contracts: Faculty Rights and Administrative Discretion." *Journal of Higher Education* 64(3): 312–48.

Rice, Eugene R., and Ann E. Austin. 1988. "High Faculty Morale: What Exemplary Colleges Do Right." *Change* 20(3): 50–58.

Royalty, Georgia M., and Thomas M. Magoon. 1985. "Correlates of Scholarly Productivity among Counseling Psychologists." *Journal of Counseling Psychology* 32(3): 458–61.

St. John, Edward P. 1989. "The Influence of Student Aid on Persistence." *Journal of Student Financial Aid* 19(3): 52–68.

―――. 1990a. "Price Response in Enrollment Decisions: An Analysis of the High School and Beyond Sophomore Cohort." *Research in Higher Education* 31(2): 161–76.

―――. 1990b. "Price Response in Persistence Decisions: An Analysis of the High School and Beyond Senior Cohort." *Research in Higher Education* 31(4): 387–403.

―――. 1991a. "A Framework of Reexamining State Resource-Management Strategies in Higher Education." *Journal of Higher Education* 62(3): 263–87.

―――. 1991b. "The Impact of Student Financial Aid: A Review of Recent Research." *Journal of Student Financial Aid* 21(1): 18–32.

―――. 1991c. "The Transformation of Liberal Arts Colleges: An Analysis of Selected Case Studies." *Review of Higher Education* 15(1): 83–108.

―――. 1991d. "What Really Influences Minority Attendance? Sequential Analyses of the High School and Beyond Sophomore Cohort." *Research in Higher Education* 31(4): 387–403.

―――. 1992a. "Changes in Pricing Behavior during the 1980s: An Analysis of Selected Case Studies." *Journal of Higher Education* 63(2): 165–87.

―――. 1992b. "Workable Models for Institutional Research on the Impact of Student Financial Aid." *Journal of Student Financial Aid* 22(3): 13–26.

―――. 1993a. "Toward a Faculty Role in Financial Strategy: A Critical Analysis of Retrenchment Processes in Three States." Paper prepared for the National Education Association and the Maine Education Association.

―――. 1993b. "Untangling the Web: Using Price-Response Measures in Enrollment Projections." *Journal of Higher Education* 64(6): 676–95.

―――. 1994a. "Assessing Tuition and Student Aid Strategies: Using Price-Response Measures to Simulate Pricing Alternatives." *Research in Higher Education* 35(3): 301–34.

―――. Fall 1994b. "Retrenchment: A Three-State Analysis." *Thought & Action* 10(2): 80–97.

St. John, Edward P., Sandra C. Andrieu, Jeffrey Oescher, and Johnny B. Starkey. 1994. "The Influence of Student Aid on Within-Year Persistence by Traditional College-Age Students in Four-Year Colleges." *Research in Higher Education* 35(4): 455–80.

St. John, Edward P., and Richard J. Elliott. 1994. "Reframing Policy Research: A Critical Examination of Research on Federal Student Aid Programs." In *Higher Education: Handbook of Theory and Research,* edited by J.C. Smart. Vol. 10. New York: Agathon Press.

St. John, Edward P., Rita Kirshstein, and Jay Noell. 1987. "The Effects of Student Aid on Persistence: A Sequential Analysis." Paper presented at an annual meeting of the American Educational Research Association, April, New Orleans, Louisiana.

———. 1991. "The Effects of Student Aid on Persistence: Sequential Analyses of the High School and Beyond Senior Cohort." *Review of Higher Education* 14(3): 383–406.

St. John, Edward P., and Charles L. Masten. 1990. "Return on the Federal Investment in Student Financial Aid: An Assessment of the High School Class of 1972." *Journal of Student Financial Aid* 20(3): 4–23.

St. John, Edward P., and Jay Noell. 1988. "Student Loans and Higher Education Opportunities: Evidence on Access, Persistence, and Choice of Major." In *Proceedings of the Fourth Annual NASSGP/ NCHELP Conference on Student Financial Aid Research,* June 3–5, 1987, St. Louis, Missouri. Vol. 1. Albany: New York State Higher Education Services Corp.

———. 1989. "The Impact of Financial Aid on Access: An Analysis of Progress with Special Consideration of Minority Access." *Research in Higher Education* 30(6): 563–82.

St. John, Edward P., Donald M. Norris, and Charles Byce. 1987. *Public/ Private Enrollment in Higher Education.* Prepared for the National Center for Education Statistics. Washington, D.C.: Pelavin Associates.

St. John, Edward P., Jeffrey Oescher, and Sandra C. Andrieu. 1992. "The Influence of Prices on Within-Year Persistence by Traditional College-Age Students in Four-Year Colleges." *Journal of Student Financial Aid* 22(1): 17–26.

St. John, Edward P., and Patricia Somers. *In press.* "Assessing the Impact of Student Financial Aid on First-Time Enrollment." In *Manual for Research on Student Financial Aid,* edited by J.S. Davis. Washington, D.C.: National Association of Financial Aid Administrators.

St. John, Edward P., and Johnny B. Starkey. 1994. "The Influence of Costs on Persistence by Traditional College-Age Students in Community Colleges." *Community College Journal of Research and Practice* 18(4): 201–14.

———. *In press.* "An Alternative to Net Price: Assessing the Effects of Prices and Price Subsidies on Within-Year Persistence." *Journal of Higher Education.*

St. John, Edward P., Johnny B. Starkey, Michael B. Paulsen, and Loretta Mbadugha. *In press.* "The Influence of Prices and Price Subsidies on Within-Year Persistence by Students in Proprietary Schools." *Educational Evaluation and Policy Analysis.*

Schiele, Jerome H. 1991. "Publication Productivity of African-American Social Work Faculty." *Journal of Social Work Education* 27(2): 125–34.

Schwartz, J.B. 1985. "Student Financial Aid and the College Enrollment Decision: The Effects of Grants and Interest Subsidies." *Economics of Education Review* 4(7): 129–144.

Setter, Gerald L., and Jack Rayburn. 1994. "Designing State Grant Programs: A Partnership of Students, Families, and Taxpayers." Paper presented at the 11th Annual NASSGP/NCHELP Conference on Student Financial Aid Research, April 7–9, San Francisco, California.

Seymour, Daniel T. 1993. *On Q: Causing Quality in Higher Education.* New York: ACE/Macmillan.

Shelton, William E., and Deborah DeZure. 1993. "Fostering a Teaching Culture in Higher Education." *Thought & Action* 8(2): 27–48.

Sherr, Lawrence A., and Deborah J. Teeter. 1991. *Total Quality Management in Higher Education.* San Francisco: Jossey-Bass.

Simsek, Hsan, and Richard B. Heydinger. 1992. "An Analysis of the Paradigmatic Shift in the Evolution of U.S. Higher Education and Its Implications for the Year 2000." Paper presented at an annual meeting of the Association for the Study of Higher Education. ED 352 923. 72 pp. MF–01; PC–03.

Slaughter, Sheila. 1991. "The Official 'Ideology' of Higher Education: Ironies and Inconsistencies." In *Culture and Ideology in Higher Education,* edited by W.G. Tierney. New York: Praeger.

———. 1993a. "Introduction." *Journal of Higher Education* 64(3): 247–49.

———. 1993b. "Retrenchment in the 1980s: The Politics of Prestige and Gender." *Journal of Higher Education* 64(3): 250–82.

Sloan, DeVillo. 1994. "Total Quality Management in the Culture of Higher Education." *Review of Higher Education* 17(4): 447–64.

Snyder, Thomas D. 1993. *Digest of Education Statistics: 1993.* Washington, D.C.: National Center for Education Statistics. ED 362 971. 571 pp. MF–01; PC–23.

Snyder, Thomas D., and Eva C. Galambos. 1988. *Higher Education Administrative Costs: Continuing the Study.* Washington, D.C.: National Center for Education Statistics. ED 286 460. 90 pp. MF–01; PC–04.

Somers, Patricia, and Edward P. St. John. 1993. "Assessing the Impact of Student Aid on Enrollment Decisions." *Journal of Student Financial Aid* 23(3): 7–12.

———. *In press.* "Assessing the Effects of Financial Aid on Persistence." In *Manual for Research on Student Financial Aid,* edited by Jerry S. Davis. Washington, D.C.: National Association of Student Financial Aid Administrators.

Southern Association of Colleges and Schools. 1992. *Criteria for Accreditation Commission on Colleges: 1992–93.* Decatur, Ga.: Author.

State Higher Education Executive Officers, Committee on College Costs. 1988. "Report on the Costs of College to Students." Denver: Author. ED 299 875. 15 pp. MF–01; PC–01.

Steeples, Douglas W. 1988a. "Westminster College of Salt Lake." In *Successful Strategic Planning: Case Studies,* edited by Douglas W. Steeples. New Directions in Higher Education No. 64. San Francisco: Jossey-Bass.

———, ed. 1988b. *Successful Strategic Planning: Case Studies.* New Directions in Higher Education No. 64. San Francisco: Jossey-Bass.

Swain, Donald C. 1988. "The University of Louisville." In *Successful Strategic Planning: Case Studies,* edited by Douglas W. Steeples. New Directions in Higher Education No. 64. San Francisco: Jossey-Bass.

Terkla, Dawn G. 1985. "Does Financial Aid Enhance Undergraduate Persistence?" *Journal of Student Financial Aid* 15(3): 11–18.

Tierney, Michael L. 1980a. "The Impact of Student Financial Aid on Student Demand for Public/Private Higher Education." *Journal of Higher Education* 45(1): 89–125.

———. Winter 1980b. "Student Matriculation Decisions and Student Aid." *Review of Higher Education* 3: 14–25.

———. July 1982. "An Estimation of Department Cost Functions." *Higher Education* 9: 453–68.

Tierney, William G., ed. 1991. *Culture and Ideology in Higher Education: Advancing a Critical Agenda.* New York: Praeger.

———. 1992. "An Anthropological Analysis of Student Participation in College." *Journal of Higher Education* 63(6): 603–18.

———. 1993. "Academic Freedom and the Parameters of Knowledge." *Harvard Educational Review* 63(2): 143–60.

Tinto, Vincent. 1975. "Dropout from Higher Education: A Theoretical Synthesis of Recent Research." *Review of Educational Research* 45: 89–125.

———. 1987. *Leaving College: Rethinking the Causes and Cures of College Attrition.* Chicago: Univ. of Chicago Press.

To, Duc-Le. 1987. *Estimating the Cost of a Bachelor's Degree: An Institutional Cost Analysis.* Washington, D.C.: U.S. Dept. of Education, Office of Educational Research and Improvement. ED 283 499. 98 pp. MF–01; PC–04.

Trammell, Mary L. 1994. "Using National Price-Response Measures to Estimate the Effects of Midyear Price Changes." Paper presented at the Association for Institutional Research National Forum, April 1, New Orleans, Louisiana.

Tynes, Susan F. 1993. "The Relationship of Social, Economic, Academic, and Institutional Characteristics to Persistence of Non-Traditional-Age Students in Higher Education: Implications for Counselors." Doctoral dissertation, Univ. of New Orleans.

U.S. Department of Education. ca. 1990. *Tough Choices: A Guide to Administrative Cost Management in Colleges and Universities.* Washington, D.C.: Author.

Volkwein, J. Frederick. 1987. "State Regulation and Campus Autonomy." In *Higher Education: Handbook of Theory and Research,* edited by John C. Smart. New York: Agathon.

———. 1989. "Changes in Quality among Public Colleges and Universities." *Journal of Higher Education* 60: 136–51.

Wagner, Alan P. 1987. "Comments." In *Estimating the Cost of a Bachelor's Degree: An Institutional Cost Analysis,* by Duc-Le To. Washington, D.C.: U.S. Dept. of Education, Office of Educational Research and Improvement. ED 283 499. 98 pp. MF–01; PC–04.

Wallace, Thomas P. 1992. "Public College Access and Affordability." *Journal of Student Financial Aid* 22(1): 39–41.

Washington Post. 13 August 1994. "Ivory-Tower Budgets." Editorial.

Weathersby, George B., and Fredric C. Balderston. 1971. "PPBS in Higher Education Planning and Management. Part 1, An Overview." *Higher Education* 1: 191–206.

———. 1972. *PPBS in Higher Education Planning and Management.* Report No. 51. Ford Foundation Project for Research in University Administration. Berkeley: Univ. of California Press.

Weathersby, George B., Gregory A. Jackson, Fredric Jacobs, Edward P. St. John, and Tyler Tingley. 1977. "The Development of Institutions of Higher Education: Theory and Assessment of Impact in Four Possible Areas of Federal Intervention." In *Evaluation Studies: Review Annual.* Beverly Hills, Calif.: Sage.

Weathersby, George B., and Fredric Jacobs. 1977. *Institutional Goals and Student Costs.* AAHE-ERIC Higher Education Research Report No. 2. Washington, D.C.: American Association for Higher Education. ED 136 706. 57 pp. MF–01; PC–03.

Wildavsky, Aaron. 1975. *Budgeting: A Comparative Theory of Budgetary Processes.* Boston: Little, Brown.

———. 1979. *Speaking Truth to Power: The Art and Craft of Policy Analysis.* Boston: Little, Brown.

———. 1984. *The Politics of the Budget Process.* 4th ed. Boston: Little, Brown.

Williams, Leslie. 29 October 1993. "College Is a Bargain, Analyst Says. Higher Education Is Lifetime of Higher Wages." *Times-Picayune.*

Wilms, W.W., R.W. Moore, and R.E. Bolus. 1987. "Whose Fault Default? A Study of the Impact of Student Characteristics and Institutional Practices on Guaranteed Student Loan Default Rates in California." *Educational Evaluation and Policy Analysis* 9(2): 41–54.

Wilson, Reginald. 1986. "Overview of the Issue: Minority/Poverty Student Enrollment Problems." Paper presented at the Third Annual NASSGP/NCHELP Conference on Student Financial Aid Research, Chicago, Illinois.

Wilson, Robin. 1987. "Changes in Guaranteed Loan Programs Are Slashing Sizes of Loans and Number of Students Eligible." *Chronicle of Higher Education* 34(2): A31–A32.

Winston, Gordon C. 1994. "The Decline in Undergraduate Teaching:

Moral Failure or Market Pressure?" *Change* 26(5): 8–15.

Zemsky, Robert. 1987. "Comments." In *Estimating the Cost of a Bachelor's Degree: An Institutional Cost Analysis,* by Duc-Le To. Washington, D.C.: U.S. Dept. of Education, Office of Educational Research and Improvement. ED 283 499. 98 pp. MF–01; PC–04.

Zook, Jim. 1 September 1993. "Nine Hundred Institutions Could Be Dropped from Student-Aid Programs for High Default Rates: 55 Are Nonprofit Colleges." *Chronicle of Higher Education:* A31.

———. 16 February 1994a. "Clinton Plan Could Raise Pell Grant Limit to $2,400." *Chronicle of Higher Education:* A31+.

———. 7 August 1994b. "Colleges Warned of Audits: Notices from Education Department Prompt Angry Reactions on the Campuses." *Chronicle of Higher Education:* A17.

———. 28 September 1994c. "Student-Aid Overhaul Pressed." *Chronicle of Higher Education:* A33+.

INDEX

A

academic productivity, increase of, 111–113

academic units, make more responsible for setting own tuition, 109

Accountability in Public Higher Education Advisory Committee, 103

accreditation agencies, attempts to force monitoring of loan defaults, 73–74

accrediting associations criteria, 58

"action experiments," 113, 116

action inquiry, essential for academic and administrative revitalization, 89

adaptive strategic planning, promotion of, 21

administrative lattice, 86

administrative productivity, increase of, 110–111

African Americans. *See* Blacks

American Council on Education, report of, 2, 34

assessment techniques, adopted by states for public education, 39

B

Bennett, William, 2, 8, 10, 53

Blacks. *See also* minority students

cut in state funding cause reduction in persistence of, 35–36

cuts in federal grant programs negatively affected participation, 11

enrollment of in colleges increased between 1976 and 1984, 17

few lower-achieving enroll in college, 9

human capital theory does not predict earnings correctly, 70

participation in Title IV programs, 15–16, 25

policies that limited opportunities for, 89

study of decline in participation rate through class dialectic, 77

Bowen's theory. *See* revenue theory

budget analyses, need to communicate results of to public, 97

C

California

faculty workloads and growth in administrative costs issue, 38

proposed use of quality management techniques, 107

state university system, study of the economic impact of funding, 41

Cames, Bruce, 8

centralization and quality, reverse relationship for state universities, 39

centralized strategic action, improved quality and reduced costs of, 22

G

goals of students and taxpayers not necessarily same as those of faculty, 60

H

HEGIS, 17

high-tuition, high-aid strategy for state funding, 99, 101–102

Higher Education Act Amendments of 1972
 federal institutional subsidy not funded under Title 1, 75
 subject to substantial revisions through budgetary processes, 88

Higher Education Act of 1965 Title IV programs
 change in funding over time, 13–15
 end of, 4
 human capital theory basis as argument to reauthorize, 67
 participation rates, 15–16
 programs lacked philosophical and other bases for growth, 74
 purpose of, 13
 subject to substantial revisions through budgetary processes, 88
 technical improvements in delivery of student aid, 20

Higher Education General Information Survey. *See* HEGIS

higher education as an investment, from average consumer perspective, 61–62

Hispanics. *See also* minority students
 cuts in federal grant programs negatively affected participation, 11
 participation in Title IV programs, 15–16

"historically disadvantaged," original target for federal student aid, 10

human capital formation, intermediate theory on, 79–83

human capital theory, 67–70
 theoretical claims, 68–69
 limitations, 69–70

I

incremental
 changes to federal budgets, 96–98
 policy decisions, policy studies are mechanisms for informing, 87

individuals, not institutions, should have education subsidized, 5

innovation increased by strong state centralization, 31

institutional grant allocations fuel tuition increase, 9–10

instructional cost reduction, effect of incentives of academy, 59

Intermediate Theory on policy making in higher education, 79–91

investment, return on, 99

K

Kansas, efforts to establish expenditure targets in, 84, 103

L

Liberal position on education support, 6–7, 24–25
    assessing claims of, 42
    use of human capital theory, 68
Lindblom (1977), 74
Louisiana, new group to study productivity promotion, 38, 103
low-income students
    responsive to amount of grant but not amount of
      loan, 19, 33
    negatively influenced by recent financial restructuring, 44

M

Maine, requests cuts in administrators' salaries, 38
market forces
    fueled increases in production costs, 85
    influenced changes in expenditures, 65
middle class
    programs, hardest hit by budget reductions, 40
    students victims of retrenchment, 11
    students, more responsive to loans than grants, 19, 33
Minnesota
    effect of net price theory on new financing strategy, 75
    efforts to establish expenditure targets in, 84, 103
    funding based upon full year enrollment, 105
    growth of budget line-item appropriations under new
      policy, 104
    high-tuition and high-aid strategy, 36
    one of few states attempting to address rising student
      costs, 38
minorities, poor academic preparation of, 9
minority students
    more responsive to prices and price subsidies, 79
    negatively influenced by cuts in federal grants, 25
    negatively influenced by recent financial restructuring, 44
multimedia format, use of for teaching, 112

N

National Association of College and University Business
    Officers, 86
National Center for Education Statistics, 55
National Commission on Student Financial Assistance, 52
National Commission on the Financing of Postsecondary
    Education, 75, 95
National Longitudinal Study of the High School Class of 1980, 18
National Postsecondary Student Aid Survey of 1986–87, 34

potential for improving, 82–83, 99
promotion in higher education, 19–20
public college
grants negatively associated with persistence, 34
tuition very negatively associated with persistence, 34
political incrementalism, 74–77
theoretical claims, 74–76
limitations, 76–77
value of, 76–77

Q

quality of a university, not related to strong state centralization, 31
quality of education and cost, confusion about relationship
between, 37

R

Reagan, effect of election of, 4
regulation as best means of controlling costs, idea of, 73–74
retrenchment, 4
retrenchment, impact of, 39–40
revenue theory, 8, 70–74
limitations, 73–74
theoretical claims, 70–73

S

SHEEO, 35
social interaction mode. *See* political incrementalism
standardized student price-response coefficients don't predict
enrollment, 70
State Higher Education Executive Officers. *See* SHEEO
state funding shift from institutional to student subsidies, 94–96
state regulations appear to impede quality and productivity, 43
state support of higher education, reduction of, 29–30
causes persistence decrease, 35
causes tuition increase, 10
strategic planning and management, 1
methodologies widely adapted, 45
strategic revolution, 108
student aid and enrollment, link between, 18, 25
student aid
as an investment, measurement of, 23
not effective in promoting access, 8
student choice, assessing effects of price changes on, 99
student-choice construct, as additional basis for public policy
decisions, 81
Supplemental Educational Opportunity Grant, 53
systematic reforms in federal student aid, suggested, 93–96

T

tuition raised

      because colleges and universities wasteful not valid, 64

      for private colleges, because of federal grant dollar
          loss, 64–65

      for public colleges not because of federal grant dollar
          loss, 43, 64–65

      in response to loss of state revenue, 31, 43, 65

      to attract more federal student aid, 8, 63

tuition charges rose substantially faster than inflation, 46–48

tuition and grants, linkage of, 105–106

tax returns from public support of higher education positive, 44

Tough Choices, publication of, 21, 22

      strategy proposed in, 107

tuition increase, ideological reasons for cause, 6–10

"trap of double counting," 10

U

U.S. Department of Education, 107

University of Florida, 48

University of Georgia, 48

University of Massachusetts at Boston, 41

University of Minnesota, cost-centered tuition, 36

W

Wildavsky (1979), 74

Y

Yavapai College, 112

ASHE-ERIC HIGHER EDUCATION REPORTS

Since 1983, the Association for the Study of Higher Education (ASHE) and the Educational Resources Information Center (ERIC) Clearinghouse on Higher Education, a sponsored project of the School of Education and Human Development at The George Washington University, have cosponsored the *ASHE-ERIC Higher Education Report* series. The 1994 series is the twenty-third overall and the sixth to be published by the School of Education and Human Development at the George Washington University.

Each monograph is the definitive analysis of a tough higher education problem, based on thorough research of pertinent literature and institutional experiences. Topics are identified by a national survey. Noted practitioners and scholars are then commissioned to write the reports, with experts providing critical reviews of each manuscript before publication.

Eight monographs (10 before 1985) in the ASHE-ERIC Higher Education Report series are published each year and are available on individual and subscription bases. To order, use the order form on the last page of this book.

Qualified persons interested in writing a monograph for the ASHE-ERIC Higher Education Reports are invited to submit a proposal to the National Advisory Board. As the preeminent literature review and issue analysis series in higher education, we can guarantee wide dissemination and national exposure for accepted candidates. Execution of a monograph requires at least a minimal familiarity with the ERIC database, including *Resources in Education* and *Current Index to Journals in Education.* The objective of these Reports is to bridge conventional wisdom with practical research. Prospective authors are strongly encouraged to call Dr. Fife at 800-773-3742.

For further information, write to
ASHE-ERIC Higher Education Reports
The George Washington University
1 Dupont Circle, Suite 630
Washington, DC 20036
Or phone (202) 296-2597, toll-free: 800-773-ERIC.
Write or call for a complete catalog.

ADVISORY BOARD

Scott Rickard
Association of College Unions–International

G. Jeremiah Ryan
Harford Community College

Patricia A. Spencer
Riverside Community College

Frances Stage
Indiana University–Bloomington

Ellen Switkes
University of California–Oakland

Barbara E. Taylor
Association of Governing Boards

Carolyn J. Thompson
State University of New York–Buffalo

Sheila L. Weiner
Board of Overseers of Harvard College

Richard A. Yanikoski
De Paul University

REVIEW PANEL

Charles Adams
University of Massachusetts–Amherst

Louis Albert
American Association for Higher Education

Richard Alfred
University of Michigan

Henry Lee Allen
University of Rochester

Philip G. Altbach
Boston College

Marilyn J. Amey
University of Kansas

Kristine L. Anderson
Florida Atlantic University

Karen D. Arnold
Boston College

Robert J. Barak
Iowa State Board of Regents

Alan Bayer
Virginia Polytechnic Institute and State University

John P. Bean
Indiana University–Bloomington

John M. Braxton
Peabody College, Vanderbilt University

Ellen M. Brier
Tennessee State University

Barbara E. Brittingham
The University of Rhode Island

Dennis Brown
University of Kansas

Peter McE. Buchanan
Council for Advancement and
    Support of Education

Patricia Carter
University of Michigan

John A. Centra
Syracuse University

Arthur W. Chickering
George Mason University

Darrel A. Clowes
Virginia Polytechnic Institute and State University

Deborah M. DiCroce
Piedmont Virginia Community College

Cynthia S. Dickens
Mississippi State University

Sarah M. Dinham
University of Arizona

Kenneth A. Feldman
State University of New York–Stony Brook

Dorothy E. Finnegan
The College of William & Mary

Mildred Garcia
Montclair State College

Rodolfo Z. Garcia
Commission on Institutions of Higher Education

Kenneth C. Green
University of Southern California

James Hearn
University of Georgia

Edward R. Hines
Illinois State University

Bruce Anthony Jones
University of Pittsburgh

Elizabeth A. Jones
The Pennsylvania State University

George D. Kuh
Indiana University–Bloomington

Daniel T. Layzell
University of Wisconsin System

Patrick G. Love
Kent State University

Cheryl D. Lovell
State Higher Education Executive Officers

Meredith Jane Ludwig
American Association of State Colleges and Universities

Dewayne Matthews
Western Interstate Commission for Higher Education

Mantha V. Mehallis
Florida Atlantic University

James R. Mingle
State Higher Education Executive Officers

John A. Muffo
Virginia Polytechnic Institute and State University

L. Jackson Newell
University of Utah

James C. Palmer
Illinois State University

Robert A. Rhoads
The Pennsylvania State University

G. Jeremiah Ryan
Harford Community College

Mary Ann Danowitz Sagaria
The Ohio State University

Daryl G. Smith
The Claremont Graduate School

Carolyn Thompson
State University of New York–Buffalo

William G. Tierney
University of Southern California

Susan B. Twombly
University of Kansas

Robert A. Walhaus
University of Illinois–Chicago

Harold Wechsler
University of Rochester

Elizabeth J. Whitt
University of Illinois–Chicago

Michael J. Worth
The George Washington University

RECENT TITLES

1994 ASHE-ERIC Higher Education Reports

1. The Advisory Committee Advantage: Creating an Effective Strategy for Programmatic Improvement
   by Lee Teitel

2. Collaborative Peer Review: The Role of Faculty in Improving College Teaching
   by Larry Keig and Michael D. Waggoner

1993 ASHE-ERIC Higher Education Reports

1. The Department Chair: New Roles, Responsibilities and Challenges
   Alan T. Seagren, John W. Creswell, and Daniel W. Wheeler

2. Sexual Harassment in Higher Education: From Conflict to Community
   Robert O. Riggs, Patricia H. Murrell, and JoAnn C. Cutting

3. Chicanos in Higher Education: Issues and Dilemmas for the 21st Century
   by Adalberto Aguirre, Jr., and Ruben O. Martinez

4. Academic Freedom in American Higher Education: Rights, Responsibilities, and Limitations
   by Robert K. Poch

5. Making Sense of the Dollars: The Costs and Uses of Faculty Compensation
   by Kathryn M. Moore and Marilyn J. Amey

6. Enhancing Promotion, Tenure and Beyond: Faculty Socialization as a Cultural Process
   by William G. Tierney and Robert A. Rhoads

7. New Perspectives for Student Affairs Professionals: Evolving Realities, Responsibilities and Roles
   by Peter H. Garland and Thomas W. Grace

8. Turning Teaching Into Learning: The Role of Student Responsibility in the Collegiate Experience
   by Todd M. Davis and Patricia Hillman Murrell

1992 ASHE-ERIC Higher Education Reports

1. The Leadership Compass: Values and Ethics in Higher Education
   John R. Wilcox and Susan L. Ebbs

2. Preparing for a Global Community: Achieving an International Perspective in Higher Education
   Sarah M. Pickert

3. Quality: Transforming Postsecondary Education
   Ellen Earle Chaffee and Lawrence A. Sherr

---

4. Faculty Job Satisfaction: Women and Minorities in Peril
   Martha Wingard Tack and Carol Logan Patitu

5. Reconciling Rights and Responsibilities of Colleges and Students: Offensive Speech, Assembly, Drug Testing, and Safety
   Annette Gibbs

6. Creating Distinctiveness: Lessons from Uncommon Colleges and Universities
   Barbara K. Townsend, L. Jackson Newell, and Michael D. Wiese

7. Instituting Enduring Innovations: Achieving Continuity of Change in Higher Education
   Barbara K. Curry

8. Crossing Pedagogical Oceans: International Teaching Assistants in U.S. Undergraduate Education
   Rosslyn M. Smith, Patricia Byrd, Gayle L. Nelson, Ralph Pat Barrett, and Janet C. Constantinides

1991 ASHE-ERIC Higher Education Reports

1. Active Learning: Creating Excitement in the Classroom
   Charles C. Bonwell and James A. Eison

2. Realizing Gender Equality in Higher Education: The Need to Integrate Work/Family Issues
   Nancy Hensel

3. Academic Advising for Student Success: A System of Shared Responsibility
   Susan H. Frost

4. Cooperative Learning: Increasing College Faculty Instructional Productivity
   David W. Johnson, Roger T. Johnson, and Karl A. Smith

5. High School–College Partnerships: Conceptual Models, Programs, and Issues
   Arthur Richard Greenberg

6. Meeting the Mandate: Renewing the College and Departmental Curriculum
   William Toombs and William Tierney

7. Faculty Collaboration: Enhancing the Quality of Scholarship and Teaching
   Ann E. Austin and Roger G. Baldwin

8. Strategies and Consequences: Managing the Costs in Higher Education
   John S. Waggaman

1990 ASHE-ERIC Higher Education Reports

1. The Campus Green: Fund Raising in Higher Education
   Barbara E. Brittingham and Thomas R. Pezzullo

2. The Emeritus Professor: Old Rank - New Meaning
   James E. Mauch, Jack W. Birch, and Jack Matthews

3. "High Risk" Students in Higher Education: Future Trends
   Dionne J. Jones and Betty Collier Watson

4. Budgeting for Higher Education at the State Level: Enigma,
   Paradox, and Ritual
   Daniel T. Layzell and Jan W. Lyddon

5. Proprietary Schools: Programs, Policies, and Prospects
   John B. Lee and Jamie P. Merisotis

6. College Choice: Understanding Student Enrollment Behavior
   Michael B. Paulsen

7. Pursuing Diversity: Recruiting College Minority Students
   Barbara Astone and Elsa Nuñez-Wormack

8. Social Consciousness and Career Awareness: Emerging Link
   in Higher Education
   John S. Swift, Jr.

1989 ASHE-ERIC Higher Education Reports

1. Making Sense of Administrative Leadership: The 'L' Word in
   Higher Education
   Estela M. Bensimon, Anna Neumann, and Robert Birnbaum

2. Affirmative Rhetoric, Negative Action: African-American and
   Hispanic Faculty at Predominantly White Universities
   Valora Washington and William Harvey

3. Postsecondary Developmental Programs: A Traditional Agenda
   with New Imperatives
   Louise M. Tomlinson

4. The Old College Try: Balancing Athletics and Academics in
   Higher Education
   John R. Thelin and Lawrence L. Wiseman

5. The Challenge of Diversity: Involvement or Alienation in the
   Academy?
   Daryl G. Smith

6. Student Goals for College and Courses: A Missing Link in Assessing and Improving Academic Achievement
   Joan S. Stark, Kathleen M. Shaw, and Malcolm A. Lowther

7. The Student as Commuter: Developing a Comprehensive Institutional Response
   Barbara Jacoby

8. Renewing Civic Capacity: Preparing College Students for Service and Citizenship
   Suzanne W. Morse

1988 ASHE-ERIC Higher Education Reports

1. The Invisible Tapestry: Culture in American Colleges and Universities
   George D. Kuh and Elizabeth J. Whitt

2. Critical Thinking: Theory, Research, Practice, and Possibilities
   Joanne Gainen Kurfiss

3. Developing Academic Programs: The Climate for Innovation
   Daniel T. Seymour

4. Peer Teaching: To Teach is To Learn Twice
   Neal A. Whitman

5. Higher Education and State Governments: Renewed Partnership, Cooperation, or Competition?
   Edward R. Hines

6. Entrepreneurship and Higher Education: Lessons for Colleges, Universities, and Industry
   James S. Fairweather

7. Planning for Microcomputers in Higher Education: Strategies for the Next Generation
   Reynolds Ferrante, John Hayman, Mary Susan Carlson, and Harry Phillips

8. The Challenge for Research in Higher Education: Harmonizing Excellence and Utility
   Alan W. Lindsay and Ruth T. Neumann

ORDER FORM

Quantity   **Amount**

_____ Please begin my subscription to the 1994 *ASHE-ERIC Higher Education Reports* at $98.00, 31% off the cover price, starting with Report 1, 1994. Includes shipping. _____

_____ Please send a complete set of the 1993 *ASHE-ERIC Higher Education Reports* at $98.00, 31% off the cover price. Please add shipping charge, below. _____

Individual reports are avilable at the following prices:
1993 and 1994, $18.00; 1988–1992, $17.00; 1980–1987, $15.00

SHIPPING CHARGES
For orders of more than 50 books, please call for shipping information.

	1st three books	*Ea. addl. book*
U.S., 48 Contiguous States		
Ground:	$3.75	$0.15
2nd Day*:	8.25	1.10
Next Day*:	18.00	1.60
Alaska & Hawaii (2nd Day Only)*:	13.25	1.40

U.S. Territories and Foreign Countries: Please call for shipping information.
*Order will be shipping within 24 hours of request.
All prices shown on this form are subject to change.

PLEASE SEND ME THE FOLLOWING REPORTS:

Quantity	Report No.	Year	Title	Amount

Please check one of the following:
☐ Check enclosed, payable to GWU–ERIC.
☐ Purchase order attached ($45.00 minimum).
☐ Charge my credit card indicated below:
  ☐ Visa   ☐ MasterCard

Subtotal: _____
Shipping: _____
Total Due: _____

Expiration Date _____

Name _____

Title _____

Institution _____

Address _____

City _____ State _____ Zip _____

Phone _____ Fax _____ Telex _____

Signature _____ Date _____

SEND ALL ORDERS TO: ASHE-ERIC Higher Education Reports
The George Washington University
One Dupont Cir., Ste. 630, Washington, DC 20036-1183
Phone: (202) 296-2597 • Toll-free: 800-773-ERIC